"This book is well worth the wait. I recommend it to all who search for God, all who have found Him, and all who seek a deeper knowledge of Him."

—**Jill Briscoe**, best-selling author, ministry leader, and popular Bible teacher

"Intellectually satisfying and spiritually affirming, *Permission to Doubt* is a must-read for the skeptical mind and the emotionally weary. You will be led beyond answers to the ultimate prize of a solid faith you can bank on."

—**Micca Campbell**, Proverbs 31 Ministry speaker and author, *An Untroubled Heart*

"In *Permission to Doubt*, Ann provides compelling answers to many of the most significant questions related to mankind's purpose and design. Her writing rises to a level warranted by the importance of those questions. It's a challenging and rewarding read."

—**Dr. Gene A. Getz**, president, Center for Church Renewal, Plano, Texas

"Ann C. Sullivan's success as a public orator stems from her wit, sincerity, wide range of knowledge, and genuine love of her audience. She now brings these same skills and experience to the writing of *Permission to Doubt*. This isn't a textbook; it's a visit with a woman who teaches, shares, and encourages."

—**Dr. Dennis E. Hensley**, author, *Jesus in the 9 to 5*

"If you have ever doubted your faith, questioned a biblical principle, or wondered if there really is a God, read this book. In *Permission to Doubt*, Ann Sullivan dares to ask the hard questions while simultaneously revealing her own journey through doubt. This book is filled with relevant biblical truth, riveting illustrations, and transformational principles. You probably already know five people who need this book. I highly recommend it."

—**Carol Kent**, speaker and author,
Unquenchable: Grow a Wildfire Faith That Will Endure Anything

"People who think can't help it. They simply need to ask the who, what, why, where, and how questions as they hear theories, ideas, and opinions along their journey of living their ordinary yet reflective and intensely personal lives. Formulas and religious mantras frustrate them like a 'one size fits all' garment or tool. It is for such Christian seekers and would-be followers of Christ that Ann Sullivan has shared her quest for a faith that satisfies. All the answers don't come at once but are ultimately to be found in a confident and persistent search for the God of the Scriptures. This is truly a helpful book for those who are too honest to be satisfied by hollow bromides and platitudes, even those offered by well-meaning Christians. Read it. You will be glad you did."

—**Jay Kesler**, president emeritus, Taylor University

"When doubt plagues us, we can believe that God has done something wrong to cause our skittish reaction. Privately, we back up and rarely admit that we are keeping God at arm's length. The subject of doubt is not usually addressed in all its complexities. It needs to be, and Ann Sullivan has done it. In the process, she does not minimize its causes or its devastations. There is no way to read this without doing some valuable, Spirit-led, rugged introspection. No need to fear the journey, however. God's Word is an anchor that holds anyone fast in the most severe storm of doubt. This book is a valuable resource and you can be sure I'll be passing it along."

—**Christine Wyrtzen**, founder and director, Daughters of Promise

PERMISSION TO DOUBT

PERMISSION TO DOUBT

One Woman's Journey *into a* Thinking Faith

Ann C. Sullivan

Kregel
Publications

Published by Kregel Publications, a division of Kregel, Inc.,
2450 Oak Industrial Drive NE, Grand Rapids, MI 49505.

ISBN 978-0-8254-4366-4

Printed in the United States of America
14 15 16 17 18 / 5 4 3 2 1

For Sully

Doubt is a pain too lonely to know
that faith is his twin brother.

Khalil Gibran

CONTENTS

Acknowledgments

This book has been a long time in coming, as family and friends can attest. Several years ago, when two publishers approached me about writing, which is the natural next step for a speaker, I was thrilled. But I also knew I wasn't ready. Not only did I need more time to process life, I also needed to figure out why I so often agreed with the skeptics of my faith.

When it was finally time to take the plunge, I knew I needed to find unbiased people who could perform the delicate task of offering honest feedback without destroying me. Four editors were instrumental.

Tom Cox from Whitaker House began the first leg of the race by reminding me that he reads many manuscripts, and while it can get torturous at times, mine was a pleasure to review. Next to grab the baton was Mattie Wolfe of Crossway who took me to coffee and said, "You really have something special here. Don't give up." The third leg of the race brought me to the amazing Dennis E. "Doc" Hensley—professor, author, speaker, editor, encourager . . . I'll stop there, lest I run out of room. Finally, Diana Savage, another author, editor, techy, and immensely gifted woman, brought my manuscript to the doorstep of Kregel. Thank you for being my go-to girl! If at any point these editors questioned my abilities or wondered if I'd ever taken a language arts class in my life, they never said so.

My next good fortune was to meet my agent, Les Stobbe, whose keen insight, matched only by his stellar reputation and experience in the business, gave me the confidence every new writer sorely needs.

Laying the groundwork for all of this were several spiritual giants in my life. Dr. Jay Kesler and Dr. Stuart Briscoe exposed me to deep, rational thought and balanced theological and philosophical insights with a vision that was never convoluted by extremism, legalism, or sentimentality. Both of them, along with my intensely gifted mentor, Jill Briscoe, encouraged me to grow and pursue truth in every way. I thank my parents for leading me to all of them.

None of this would have been possible, however, without one amazing internist. Dr. Tim McAvoy singlehandedly changed my life by diagnosing and treating a heart condition that had fueled a mysterious panic disorder I'd struggled with for more than a decade. His incredible insight, tempered only by his astonishing listening skills, made him the perfect doctor. Thus, he was instrumental in moving me from panic attacks to public speaking.

Thank you, family and friends. You know who you are. Thank you for loving me, supporting me, and leaving the words, "To whom much is given, much is required" ringing in my ears. It's my privilege to give back what was generously shared with me.

INTRODUCTION

Imagine having to stand up in front of hundreds of women to give a talk on "Confident Living" while struggling with serious doubt. Such was the task I faced several years ago, and as I sat at my desk poring over my notes, overwhelmed by inadequacy, I remember thinking, *Who am I to talk about confidence?*

Then it hit me: *Who better?* Who would I rather listen to address the issue of assurance: someone who has never struggled with it, or someone who has had to claw her way through a maze to find it? Don't try to sell me exercise equipment a twenty-two-year-old airbrushed model is using. Show me a middle-aged mother of four who's successfully fighting gravity, and then I'll listen.

Doubt and I go way back. We have a long history together, and our struggle has been fierce. As a speaker, though, I have doubt to thank for uniquely equipping me to address this topic. I speak to women across the country whose struggle with doubt is as real as mine was and who are relieved finally to come clean. I remind them that while doubt terrifies us in a way nothing else can, it need not signal the end of faith. Sometimes it's just the beginning. So let's give ourselves permission to doubt.

PART ONE

Doubts, Dry Spells, and the Rediscovery of Faith

Truth never lost ground by enquiry.
William Penn

Chapter 1

DEFINING TRUTH

On a college campus, years ago, I made the frigid January trek back to my dorm room. As I stepped inside, I felt lightheaded with the sensation that a weight was pulling me down. My pulse raced, my breathing became labored, and sheer terror coursed through me.

I was nineteen, and up to that point had been coasting through life quite comfortably. Although in retrospect I realize there had been signs, it wasn't until that moment of terror I finally realized I had a problem.

The panic attacks increased in both frequency and intensity, and within a month I was crippled by a full-fledged panic disorder that I would attempt to conceal for more than a decade. Doctors were at a loss to dig up a source, and counselors were baffled. I didn't fit the mold. I was healthy and well-adjusted and had grown up completely untouched by divorce and dysfunction. I was also a Christian, and there was the rub.

People doubt. Christians doubt too. We question things that at one time seemed so deeply embedded in our belief system, we were sure nothing could shake them. But life happens, circumstances change, and suddenly the honeymoon with Jesus comes to an end. Our confidence wavers as depression and despair press in, choking the faith right out of us. *How could a good God allow this kind of pain? Didn't I pray enough? Didn't I believe enough? Maybe I was wrong.*

Some of us experience doubt because our pain no longer fits our understanding of God; others because our theology no longer accommodates our choices. Throw in some disillusionment and a touch of confusion, and the ground becomes fertile for questioning faith. Regardless of its cause, however, one fact remains: doubt always hurts.

All my life I heard well-intentioned people quote the Bible and say that Christians are called to be joyful (1 Thess. 5:16), to live by faith (2 Cor. 5:7), and to be anxious for nothing (Phil. 4:6). Yet, with each terrifying panic attack it become clear to me how short I fell as a believer. I became plagued with fear and anxiety and was forced to endure the kind of oppressive silence that comes when the answers won't. More than once I pleaded for my sanity with a God I hoped was there. *If you're really there, please, just don't let me lose my mind.*

Questions began to roll through me as though I'd never really thought about anything before. Why was I suffering? Where was God in all this? Did He even exist? Didn't He care? Years later, as I began traveling across the country as a speaker, I realized that these are the kinds of questions everyone asks, particularly when they're struggling. Adversity has a way of catapulting us into an exploration of our faith, and while I encourage the investigation *before* the bottom drops out, I do hear a collective sigh of relief whenever I speak on doubt and people discover they're not alone. Giving them permission to doubt, validate their pain, and articulate their struggle always brings a measure of comfort. Thinking and asking questions is a good thing, but challenging a belief system isn't easy. It's risky and may force us to move outside the comfortable spaces we've set up for ourselves. And who knows what we'll find there?

From the first day of my panic disorder, doubt began chipping away at my faith and set me on a course I would never have chosen for myself. But from where I stand today as a communicator and teacher, I can't think of better training. Nothing could have prepared me more than picking apart what I knew as truth and discovering for myself what was really worth clinging to and what wasn't. My journey enabled me to understand a woman's fear and look her straight in the eye and say, "I know exactly how you feel and it's okay to feel that way."

Thirteen years and many doctors and counselors later, I was finally diagnosed and treated for a heart condition that released uncontrolled adrenaline into my system, fueling my panic attacks. Through one amazing doctor, I discovered a physical cause to my psychological fall-out. This solution, however, did not surface one second before God decided it was time, and with 20/20 hindsight, it's easy to see why. It took a long time for me to figure out what God was up to in my life and what He was preparing me for. Of the two kinds of speakers—those who have something to say and those who have to say something—He made sure I was the former. My battle left me with two unwavering convictions. First, there are different kinds of doubt, and each one calls for its own unique response. Second, doubt does not necessarily signal the end of faith; sometimes it is just the beginning—the perfect opportunity for faith to be strengthened.

The Truth About Truth

Stephen Board of InterVarsity Press and author of the book *Doubt* made a statement many years ago that proved to be true not only in my own life but also in the lives of the women I speak to. He said those who've never really doubted have never really believed. He's known many Christians, himself included, whose deepest convictions have grown out of personal struggle with serious doubt.

Currently, we have an entire generation of Christians who have grown up in the church, as I did, and would technically classify themselves as "believers," but are now staying away in droves. There are myriad reasons for this, not the least of which is their inability to find relevancy and answers to the issues they face in the real world. Also, our society is pluralistic, accepting all beliefs as true. Why should Christians think they have an edge on the truth?

What I've discovered about genuine truth, though, is that by its own definition, it isn't relativistic. It isn't threatened by our questions and doubts, nor is it determined by culture, opinion, the size of a church building, or evangelistic programs. Its essence doesn't change. How truth is packaged, delivered, and received, however, must keep evolving, no matter how difficult we find change. Many of us have become skeptical of organized religion in general, and have found religious people pushy, stodgy, judgmental, and homophobic. But let's not confuse our distaste for certain people, styles, or out-of-date subcultures with the essence of genuine truth. What is it we *really* object to?

Neglecting to separate the issues would be a little like me talking about my grade school math teacher who emitted a strange odor. Asking for help with an equation became painful in more ways than one. So I made a decision right then and there that I would never study mathematics.

If we're honest we'll admit that often our gripe is with Christians and what they've done in the name of Christ, rather than with Christ Himself. It's hard to argue with those whose commitment to Jesus is displayed by feeding the hungry, battling human trafficking, or rescuing the planet. Granted, Jesus asks believers to be set apart and to make a difference, but He certainly doesn't ask it of unbelievers and He makes it very clear that our primary objective is always love: "By this everyone will know that you are my disciples, if you love one another" (John 13:35). Love is a truth that has no variance over time.

But some applications of truth do change and absolutely must. Professor of philosophy J. L. Schellenberg, in his latest offering entitled *Evolutionary Religion*, is right in this respect. The practice of religion evolves along with people and their unique cultures. However, ultimate truth, something Schellenberg tends to deny, does not change, whether people embrace science and reason or prefer superstition. Truth is not impacted by us. We are impacted by truth.

Dr. Bradley Wright, in his book *Christians Are Hate-Filled Hypocrites . . . and Other Lies You've been Told*, calls attention to the fact that societies change, and if the church wants to thrive in any culture, it must clear away the clutter of older cultures and adapt to where things are now. Issues like technology, places of worship, and even changes in the average marrying age can and should affect how the church functions and remains relevant. The only constant is the God they seek.

We see instances of change regularly. There was a time when the word *fundamentalist* was a positive term, referring to those who embraced fundamental truths about a particular concept. Now it's tantamount to fanatics and suicide bombers. Today, we may be put off by the term *devil* because it sounds trite and medieval. But unless we sidestep it, or blame it on a selfish gene, we're forced to confront the fallout of evil every day of our lives. The ultimate truth of the existence of evil is undeniable.

Asking the Right Questions

Questioning a belief system we have been handed isn't a bad thing. Not only can genuine truth stand up to our doubt, but questions are an integral part of growth. They help clear through the clutter of misinformation and preconceived notions that we so quickly create and draw us back to what's most important—God and the real truth He provides. How many of us have been derailed from our pursuit of genuine truth by prejudice, bias, or personal preference?

But growing pains are not called such for nothing. A book such as Reza Aslan's *The Zealot* has sold well, not because he claimed credentials that were later questioned but because as a culture we are exhausted by the fallout of intolerance. Relativism's laid-back approach to truth may not be intellectually satisfying, but it feels like a desperately needed breath of fresh air—a release from the bondage of strict rules that are no longer relevant. However, before we throw the proverbial baby out with the bathwater, we better ask a few more questions. The stakes are high.

The apostle Paul wasn't the most dynamic preacher of his day. He wasn't like the televangelists we're used to, with their bleached white teeth and bad comb-overs. He wasn't particularly tactful either, but he was passionate. He consistently encouraged people to think outside their comfort zone and ask questions. He instructed the church in Thessalonica to test everything (1 Thess. 5:21). Like separating wheat from chaff, truth will prevail and become strengthened in the one who does the honest asking. The apostle commended the Bereans in Acts 17:11 for their investigative skills. To the Colossians he said, "See to it that no one takes you captive through hollow and deceptive philosophy, which depends on human tradition and the elemental spiritual forces of this world rather than on Christ" (Col. 2:8).

There's always been a current of truth flowing through humanity causing us to ask the big questions. Why are we here? Is there a God? Is He detached or is He engaged? Does God move us only like we might be moved by a beautiful piece of art, as Aristotle contended? Or is He Calvin's God, ruling the individual parts of the world by a providential hand?

Paul is encouraging us to keep our minds engaged and ask the questions that confront us. It's good to stretch ourselves and ponder the big questions, even the ones we can't answer, because whether our perspectives are eternal or temporal, getting truth right is too important to who we are to settle for being half true.

There are questions we may discover answers to as well, if we'll simply ask. Today's emerging church, which asks how to "do church" in postmodern culture, has become an essential part of the healthy dialogue, but not without making a few people uneasy in the process. Comfortable complacency can be much easier to live with than facing divided opinion.

Dr. Scot McKnight is an insightful New Testament scholar and historian who regularly challenges believers to think outside the box, even with regard to something as basic as how we approach the Scriptures.

In his book, *The Blue Parakeet: Rethinking How You Read the Bible,* McKnight dares to suggest that whether we're aware of it or not, we all do our fair share of "picking and choosing" when it comes to interpreting and applying what we read. He does a good job of encouraging believers to carefully separate negotiables from nonnegotiables.

History teaches us that while people and opinions come and go—along with values, societies, trends, and traditions—truth will stand forever, keeping a person rooted, less likely to be "tossed back and forth" (Eph. 4:14). All humans, including those of us in the church, tend to be uncomfortable with change. There was a time when the church was quite opposed to a heliocentric position, convinced that the sun rotated around the earth; are there areas where the church is once again blocking beneficial change because it fears the unknown? McKnight, along with many other church leaders of today, would encourage us to consider the possibility that changes may be necessary. And I agree. If the questions that accompany doubt and skepticism can usher in the kind of investigation that allows faith to flourish in truth, they have done their job.

Because They Said So

Years ago, apologist Paul Little told an amusing story about a Sunday school teacher who asked his class, "What is faith?" A little boy raised his hand and said, "Faith is believing in something you know is not true." This story, though mildly amusing at first, becomes considerably less so as we begin to struggle with doubt. We become the little boy in the story and wonder what our faith is really built on. Is it wishful thinking? Is it self-deception? We may begin to wonder why we ever believed in the first place.

Growing up in a Christian home had been a blessing and a comfort up to the point of my first struggle with doubt. Suddenly, it seemed more of a liability. What were the odds, I wondered, that of all the places in the world I could have been born, I just happened to be born into a home that had an edge on the truth? Was I one of the chosen few? Had God rejected the rest, as some held? I wasn't sure I was interested in a God who would create an entire race of people and cast the majority of them into hell.

As a university student away from home for the first time, exploring other cultures and beliefs, my faith began feeling dangerously inadequate, narrow-minded, and naïve. It wasn't as though I wanted it that way. I wasn't looking to make waves or get into heated debates like some of my classmates and philosophy professors. But I didn't want to delude myself either, pinning my hopes on something that wasn't real. I was hungry for truth and I needed answers, though I would have given anything not to have the questions in the first place.

I remember visiting my mother-in-law one afternoon soon after I graduated from college. I was still troubled by my doubts and looking for some kind of comfort, so I decided to broach the subject with her. She was an extraordinary person who was blessed with a cheery disposition and rarely complained . . . though, from where I stood, I could have pointed out to her lots of reasons she could. She had grown up in her faith, was reared in parochial school, and rarely missed church. On that particular day, as my secret storm raged within me, I asked her if she ever questioned her faith. I watched for her reaction as she stood folding laundry still warm from the dryer. She paused, looked at me, and said, "No . . . never. We were taught not to ask questions." Then, she resumed her chore contentedly as I sat in amazement, wondering why I couldn't be more like her. Why was I tortured with so many questions? Why couldn't I be satisfied with someone else doing my thinking for me?

Most of us spend the first decade of our lives believing everything our parents tell us. Up to that point, we typically trust them and take what they say at face value. In the second decade, things tend to change dramatically. Not only do we begin to challenge what our parents tell us, but we sometimes wonder if they've ever had a clue. It's almost a rite of passage, I think to myself, every time I remind my kids how cool I was before they came along.

According to child psychologists, the eventuality of separating is viewed not only as normal but as a healthy sign of developing independence. The process of separating from our parents, at least on some levels, and learning to think for ourselves are essential parts of growing up. Exactly when this happens, however, will be as different as the children themselves.

I was closing in on twenty when it happened to me. My older sister had been about eight. She trusted our parents and loved them too, but from a very early age she was an independent thinker. If something didn't make sense to her, she questioned it. I, on the other hand, the one born with the "tell me I'm good" sign taped to my back, found disagreeing with our parents unthinkable. This kind of child may make for easy parenting, but compliant acceptance can set up all sorts of future challenges for both parent and child.

I was nineteen when my sister walked into my room and asked why I was crying. When I told her my dad had said some things I didn't agree with, she looked at me knowingly and asked, "Has it ever occurred to you that Dad might actually be wrong?" I stood there, realizing for the first time that no, it had not. I pondered for a few moments this strange new concept to which my sister was introducing me. It felt a bit disquieting at first but strangely liberating.

Whether we are aware of it or not, every one of us is a product of our parents and upbringing. We are a product of our environment, our siblings, and our playground experiences. Experts have long held the position that both nature and nurture play integral roles in our development and impact every aspect of our lives, including our ability to trust.

This is so important that whenever I'm speaking on challenging life topics such as contentment, discernment, self-control, or self-image, I'm extremely careful to point out that we don't come to the table on equal footing. The ground may be level at the foot of the cross, as the old evangelical saying goes, because we all fall short of God's glory. It's level, because no matter how great or small our infraction, His grace covers it all. However, while "salvation" is equally available to everyone, not everyone has the same opportunities to understand or experience life in the same way.

Each one of us is different and will struggle with different things. Having two kids showed me that. My son came out of the womb with his little scrunched face asking, "How can I please you, Mommy?" My daughter came out asking, "Who's in charge here?" Matt seemed relaxed, wrapped up tight in his newborn blanket, but Lissy was on edge and almost too alert from her very first breath. We'd soon realize that her gigantic blue eyes weren't simply looking around the nursery . . . they were casing the joint. As I've watched my kids grow, I've recognized how the different dispositions they were assigned at birth have impacted every aspect of their lives. Their natural tendencies are powerful forces of nature and have become a crucial part of their personal equation. This in turn impacts everything about them, including how they approach, process, and challenge truth.

Nurture is just as important as nature, however. I was reared by two great parents who could not have been more different, and those differences made for quite the adventure. When life got tough, my mom, the eternal optimist, would say things like, "Do your best and pray about it. It will all work out." And, essentially, she was right. My dad, on the other hand, who'd like to think he's just as positive as my mom, was instead the ultimate pragmatist . . . which is code for Debbie Downer. In order to equip me to meet life's harsh realities, he was known to whisper things more like, "If you're ever destitute, homeless, and sleeping on a park bench . . . just remember, newspaper is excellent insulation."

It took me a long time to realize that these two factions were forever waging war in my head. Even now, I catch myself bracing for disaster and straining to hear the other shoe drop, believing the adage that if everything is going your way, you're probably driving in the wrong lane. I've never understood people who look into the news camera after some tragedy and say, "I never thought this could happen to me." I've wondered if I'll be the first to say, "I knew this was going to happen." Yet, along with all this pessimism is a strong vein of optimism. In fact, I'll have just as many moments where I'm so optimistic I frighten myself.

No matter what your upbringing, at some point we have to come to terms with our DNA, our parents, our experiences, and any other truth claims that may be at war within us. I know my parents did their best, and I've benefited from their differences, learning to temper faith with reason. I have them and my kids to thank for teaching me that our propensity to doubt and question can be as woven into our fabric as the color of our eyes. I call it the DNA of doubting. We may live an entire lifetime with a *Lord, I believe; help me in my unbelief*[1] disposition simply because our bent is to wonder if anything can be true. One minute logic tells us God is there, the next minute we're not even sure if *we* are there. I've learned that in those moments, it may have to come down to taking the risk of examining the evidence and weighing our options.

In his book, *Seeking Allah, Finding Jesus*, Dr. Nabeel Qureshi, a former devout Muslim, tells of his search for spiritual truth. Through his research and historical reasoning, he came to realize that the claims of Christ were much different from what he'd been led to believe. He now travels the world lecturing and encouraging people to investigate all the evidence and understand for themselves the differences between Jesus, Muhammad, and all the others. And though the truth has set him free, Qureshi paid a steep price by alienating a family he deeply loves. Only recently have those broken bridges begun to be rebuilt.

As I began to investigate the claims of Christ and tried to separate fact from fiction, I too knew it might lead me away from the beliefs of my youth. There are lots of things we hear growing up that should probably be given a second thought. Many of them are pretty innocuous. Turns out you won't catch a cold from simply stepping outside with a wet head. Crossing your eyes won't make them stick that way. Swimming less than an hour after eating won't make you drown.

None of these are very significant in and of themselves, but they do illustrate that not everything our parents, teachers, or pastors tell us is genuine truth. And though I don't think most of them set out to lie, they are human and, as such, are open to making mistakes. I was pretty sure my family wouldn't disown me for questioning the faith I grew up with, but I needed to brace myself, not knowing if my discoveries would prove them wrong. I knew it could be painful to disagree with them, but I also knew I'd never find comfort living on autopilot.

With that in mind let's give ourselves permission to doubt because questions are not just a good thing; they are essential to uncovering genuine truth. When it comes to dealing with doubt effectively, understanding who we are and where we're coming from is half the battle. The other half involves understanding the nature of doubt and how it attaches itself to us. When we've done that, we're ready to chart a course toward becoming who we were intended to be. So, ask away. And rest assured, truth won't break under the bright lights of interrogation.

Looking Deeper

1. How do you define truth?
2. Who has had the greatest impact—positively and negatively—on your ability to trust?
3. What events most shaped your faith?

Chapter 2

THE MYSTERY OF FAITH

As Paul Little puts it in *Know Why You Believe*, it is not enough for us to know *what* we believe; we also need to know *why* we believe it. This is great advice not only when it comes to faith but also as it pertains to doubt. It's not enough for us to know *what* we doubt without knowing *why* we doubt it.

In *The God Delusion,* evolutionary biologist and outspoken atheist Richard Dawkins says that it's impossible to make people believe something they don't. I agree. We can set up good arguments, provide empirical evidence, and debate a number of issues, but in the end no one can make a person believe something he simply doesn't. How many *true* converts were added because of the Spanish Inquisition? What Dawkins probably doesn't realize is that Scripture teaches essentially the same thing: "But the natural man does not receive the things of the Spirit of God, for they are foolishness to him; nor can he know them, because they are spiritually discerned" (1 Cor. 2:14 NKJV). The apostle Paul says no one can accept the gospel of Christ until God opens their eyes. Without that spiritual discernment, the entire message will seem irrational. And no good arguments or empirical data will change their point of view.

Jesus built on this by pointing out that God "draws" us to Himself and "enables" us to believe (John 6:44, 65). However, the tension begins when we discover that while we cannot believe without God's enabling, Scripture also teaches we will be held accountable for not believing. Jesus says, "Whoever believes in him is not condemned, but whoever does not believe stands condemned already" (John 3:18). How can this be fair? And which comes first: God enabling us to believe or our desire to believe?

Which Comes First?

There are obviously many layers to the answer to this question. In fact, one of the layers is unfolded in Luke 16, where Jesus told a parable about a rich man and a beggar. The beggar died and was carried to Abraham's side, while the rich man, who also died, was buried and found himself in hell. In his misery, the rich man pleaded with "Father Abraham" and asked if he might be permitted to go warn his five brothers what awaited them if they too rejected God's truth. Abraham responded by telling the rich man that it wouldn't make a difference: "If they do not listen to Moses and the Prophets, they will not be convinced even if someone rises from the dead" (v. 31).

Jesus' parable challenges the adage that "seeing is believing." There were plenty of people who saw Jesus in His day, and didn't believe. Although you don't necessarily need to see to believe. Most of us believe in Julius Caesar, though we've never seen him. Perhaps "living by faith and not by sight" is more complex than it sounds. But the question remains: How can God hold us accountable for a choice we make without His help?

Is our belief in Christ what changes us, or does the fact that we believe reflect the change that has already begun? Catholics and Protestants love to split hairs on this one. But the answer might just be, yes. Which in some ways might sound like a cop-out, but it is merely a study in perspective.

When my first child was born, my mortality suddenly became an issue for me. The need to care for my son was a strong maternal instinct, and I felt that if the time of my death was truly in God's hands, I could rest assured that if He took me He'd provide for the child I'd committed to Him. So, I asked my pastor, when a person dies, do they die of natural causes or does the Lord take them? He looked me straight in the eye and said, yes.

That was when God's unfathomable sovereignty became real to me. He allows freedom, but maintains control at the same time. From our perspective, all we see are the physical causes of death—old age, car accidents, or cancer. But from God's perspective, things are very different. Of God, Job states, "A person's days are determined; you have decreed the number of his months and have set limits he cannot exceed" (Job 14:5).

If you were to ask a husband about his pursuit of his wife, he might tell you all about how he sent flowers or asked her on a date. As far as he is concerned, he chose her. But to the wife, she'll tell you how she ignored him for over a year until she decided that he was a good friend and she'd like to go out on a date with him. To her, she chose him. So who started the relationship? Who chose whom?

Questions about how faith works follow a similar pattern. Is belief a matter of understanding the truth or desiring the truth? Is it possible for people to accept something they don't understand or understand something they don't accept? Do people believe because they want to or because they are compelled to? According to Scripture, the answer is yes.

Confidence in Faith

In grade school, I had a friend who lived next door whose dad was a dentist. One day I went to her house with a pocket full of bubble gum and asked her if she wanted a piece. I'll never forget her response: "My dad doesn't believe in gum."

Amazed at her words, I stood there wondering how a grown man could not believe in gum. I pointed to my bulging pocket and suggested we go show him.

Eventually I realized what my friend was saying. Her dad had made a choice about believing in gum. He didn't chew gum, nor did he promote gum chewing in any way. I'm not sure if the invention of sugar-free Trident eventually made a difference, but at the time, it was a little confusing.

Since then I've thought how believing the truth of Christ can feel just as confusing. How can two people hear the same message about the love of Christ and one get it and the other so completely not? Does believing mean we understand the truth, or does it mean we embrace it? Can we do one without the other? There are a lot of reasons why someone does or does not understand or embrace a particular concept. As I stated before, personal experiences, preconceived notions, or misinformation all contribute to how a person responds to any truth claim.

It may surprise someone who's struggling with doubt to realize that faith, from the beginning, was meant to bring strength and comfort, not confusion. However, with our terrifying free will, we humans have a great propensity for muddying the waters. Perhaps the question isn't whether or not there is genuine truth, but rather how willing we are to honestly pursue truth.

The prophet Jeremiah, known for his sobering messages to Israel, one day wrote an uncharacteristically positive bit of prose. The Old Testament's weeping prophet, as he came to be known, spoke of the confidence God's people could have if they put their trust in Him: "But blessed is the one who trusts in the LORD, whose confidence is in him" (Jer. 17:7).

In the New Testament, the apostle John built on this same theme, explaining that one of the reasons he penned his epistle in the first place was so God's people would *know* they have eternal life and have confidence in their relationship with Him: "This is the confidence we have in approaching God" (1 John 5:14). However, in the autonomous world in which we live, relationships are not without obstacles—even our relationship with God—and they can threaten the very intimacy and confidence we were intended to enjoy. In part two, we'll sort through some of the challenges to this relationship and weigh our options for finding the confidence of faith God intended for us.

Looking Deeper

1. Where does your truth originate?
2. How have you challenged your own truth claims?
3. How has that challenge impacted your life and faith?

THE THREE SIDES OF DOUBT—SPIRITUAL, INTELLECTUAL, EMOTIONAL

Unthinking faith is a curious offering to be made
to the creator of the human mind.

John A. Hutchinson

Chapter 3

SPIRITUAL DOUBT

Doubt strikes in different ways and for different reasons, typically manifesting itself spiritually, intellectually, and/or emotionally. If faith involved only one of the three we could ignore the others, but it doesn't. So, learning to recognize the different types of doubt becomes essential if we want to learn from our struggles. Os Guinness, in *God in the Dark*, says, "Doubt is not simply intellectual, an abstract philosophical or theological question. Nor is it merely psychological, a state of morbid spiritual or psychological anxiety. Doubt is personal."[1] Without question, it's the inextricable blend of mind, body, and spirit that allows doubt's steely grip to become not only personal but painful as well. As the saying goes, "One always catches the ills of the other."

Spiritual doubt, simply put, is the discomfort that surfaces because of the inability for good and evil to comfortably coexist. It typically emerges as a result of the bad choices we make, or, to put it in a less politically correct way, because of our sin. When we deliberately choose to entertain sin in our lives—lay out the welcome mat, throw it a party—we set ourselves up for all sorts of troubling and confusing consequences.

Sin has its pleasure for a season. No one denies that. Even the writer of Hebrews pointed out that it was Moses' choice to be mistreated along with God's people rather than enjoy the fleeting pleasures of sin (11:25). But like all parties, even the good ones, the celebration eventually ends, the guests leave, and all that's left is the mess. Spiritual doubt is a huge part of the mess left after the bad choices. This really shouldn't surprise us, though, because in all of Scripture God never promises peace, assurance, or personal guidance to those who celebrate sin; rather, "the LORD confides in those who fear him; he makes his covenant known to them" (Ps. 25:14).

A woman approached me at a conference several years ago, wondering why she was struggling with her life and her faith. As we visited, details of her involvement with her daughter's soccer coach emerged. Whenever they visited they felt a real connection, she said. Eventually, they started meeting alone. It wasn't exactly an affair, she insisted. Sure, there was some intimacy, but they never actually had sex. (Thank you for the clarification, President Clinton.)

When Moses delivered his instructions to God's people as they prepared to enter the land of Canaan, he acknowledged their God-given right to make their own choices . . . the same right this young mom had. Yet Moses also reminded them that within God's ordained gift of autonomy lurk some sobering consequences of bad choices. He urged them to choose wisely and receive God's best: "This day I call the heavens and the earth as witnesses against you that I have set before you life and death, blessings and curses. Now choose life, so that you and your children may live" (Deut. 30:19). Not only does Moses point out the high price of sin, but he also reminds them that in the presence of an omniscient God, any attempt to minimize their breach, or cover it up, will be futile: "Be sure that your sin will find you out" (Num. 32:23).

I reminded the young mom of this and asked her how she could expect to nurture her marriage, her family, and her walk with God, while living on the edge. Why should her faith and life feel strong when she wasn't heeding the wise adage, "When the grass looks greener in someone else's yard, water your own lawn"? I encouraged her to get the help she needed to do just that.

Our spiritual wellness will impact every area of our lives, and vice versa. Our spiritual relationship with God affects our relationships, our emotional state, our health, and so on; our relationships, health, and all the rest create consequences for our spiritual life.

In his book, *Grace for the Afflicted*, Dr. Matthew Stanford, a professor of psychology, neuroscience, and biomedical studies at Baylor University, seeks to educate the church on the topic of mental illness. He begins by identifying the spirit's connection to the body and the mind:

> It is not uncommon for neuroscientists to talk and debate about the mind. We might use fancier words like consciousness or self-awareness to make it sound more "scientific," but we are still talking about an immaterial, invisible aspect of our being. Things that can't be seen make scientists uncomfortable. We don't like to say that something is beyond our understanding or that it can't be measured. We may admit that we don't understand something presently but qualify our admission by saying that with enough study and the continued advancement of science we will one day. So to describe us as having a spirit, in addition to a mind and a body, seems almost heretical from a scientific perspective. But here is where we scientists must understand that Scripture [or God's revealed Word] is our ultimate authority and that it precisely describes our created being in the context of our relationship with God and our fellow human beings. . . .
>
> It is in our spirit that we have the opportunity to be in union with the very God of the universe.[2]

As spiritual beings, we've been given tremendous sensitivity to good and evil. In fact, the impact is so powerful that it often spills over into other areas of our lives. A classic example from history comes from the story of the second king of Israel. David committed adultery and then attempted to cover his tracks by having his impregnated mistress's husband killed. Before dealing with his sin through confession, David endured the oppression of guilt and the heavy toll it took on his mind and body:

> When I kept silent,
> > my bones wasted away
> > through my groaning all day long.
> For day and night
> > your hand was heavy on me;
> my strength was sapped
> > as in the heat of summer. (Ps. 32:3–4)

Illness is not always the direct result of our sin, but for David, in this instance, it was. And while his suffering was debilitating, his situation was far from hopeless. He had committed some serious sins, the big guys—adultery and murder—and had rationalized and compartmentalized his behavior so efficiently that by the time the prophet Nathan confronted him, he was in complete denial.

It took someone else completely, namely the prophet Nathan, to make David recognize his sin, confess it to God, and receive His forgiveness and grace. In Psalm 22, David was not only puzzled over why he was suffering, but he also was desperate to know why God wasn't stepping in to help. In verse 2 he says, "My God, I cry out by day, but you do not answer, by night, but I find no rest."

Spiritual doubt can have a direct effect on our relationships—with God as well as with those around us. There was a girl I knew in college who came from a Christian home, and though she knew better, she decided to make some bad choices. They seemed right at the time, but eventually she began feeling disconnected from God and questioning her faith.

One Sunday morning, she decided to pull herself out of bed, a monumental feat for any collegian, throw on some clothes, and drive all the way back to the church of her youth. People in general had begun to annoy her, and church people specifically. Guilt will do that to you. But somehow she remembered this church as something different, something special.

No one seemed to recognize her as she slipped in the back. She listened intently as the pastor spoke about not only the challenges of life but the high premium God places on each one of us. Quoting from 1 Corinthians 6, he pointed out that God's Spirit dwells within believers and makes their bodies His temple. The plan God has for us is to thrive spiritually, even in the midst of a physically dying world.

The reminder of this mysterious phenomenon was both comforting and convicting to my friend as she stifled tears and began considering the ways she'd been avoiding God. For the first time, she began to question some of her behaviors, including the sexual ones. Could the intimacy we too easily give away somehow compromise our intimacy with God? According to the world's standards, sexual behavior is a nonissue. The idea of changing sexual behavior by those same standards is virtually impossible. Still, as she drove back to the university, she thought of the pastor's reminder that God delights in doing the impossible. He is all about perfecting His strength in the midst of our weakness: "My grace is sufficient for you, for my power is made perfect in weakness" (2 Cor. 12:9). There was no denying that God was calling her to something else.

She determined to make changes in her life. Months of battle came to a head one night when she found herself again in the compromising situation she knew she should be avoiding. With emotions running high and hormones even higher, she felt she had no recourse but to silently cry out to the Lord for help. Suddenly, and just as mysteriously, the mood shifted as she began to have an overwhelming awareness of God's presence. It was as if Jesus were in the room, watching. A wave of resolve surged through her, as nothing can make a person button up faster than knowing Jesus is in the room. She struggled to find words to explain to her boyfriend what was happening, though she hardly understood it herself. Not sharing her conviction, particularly in that moment, he did his best to respect her decision, and the evening came to an abrupt end. The night was a complete bust, and my friend was left wondering what was wrong with her.

We live in a culture that can normalize and justify almost any behavior. Through sheer repetition and an obsession to remain "open-minded" we become desensitized to what actually might be right or wrong. We'll come back to my friend in a minute, but her story illustrates how sex has become one of those tricky subjects that we say doesn't matter and yet can cause a great deal of pain and confusion. The culture said her previous attitude toward sex was acceptable and normal, but now her spirit was being challenged by another perspective.

Several years ago, Lena Dunham burst onto the independent film scene with her movie, *Tiny Furniture.* The twentysomething filmmaker is known for her brutal honesty and the quirky characters she creates. What strikes me most about her characters, though, which are typically flailing and cast in gritty realism, is their general lack of substance and direction. Sexual encounters are often reduced to little more than any other bodily function.

Her perspective may reflect a large portion of our culture, particularly with regard to what gets pumped out of Hollywood. But as I've worked with women, both young and old, through the years, it's been my experience that even without a belief in God or a strong moral compass, the spiritual mystery of sexual intimacy, particularly when it's broken, has a far greater impact on us than we'd care to admit.

No one is suggesting we return to the days of the Puritans. But it turns out that maybe our behaviors, even the sexual ones, are worth a second look, because how we respond to these seemingly insignificant details of life may make the difference between sliding down a slippery slope that drops us into the pit of a broken family and nurturing healthy relationships with other people and God. Years ago I heard sin explained as a downward trajectory that begins with a single thought. A thought becomes a consideration. A consideration becomes an attitude. An attitude becomes an action. An action repeated long enough becomes a habit. A habit becomes a stronghold . . . a power base for the enemy.

Notice, it's not the fleeting thoughts that are the problem. It'd be hard to avoid those, without serious sedation, anyway. It's how we choose to respond to the thoughts of lust, greed, and bitterness that will make the difference. Though it should be pointed out that not everyone will be convicted in the same way with regard to right and wrong—nor will they necessarily be judged in the same way. Romans chapter 14 offers tremendous clarity with regard to that.

The apostle Paul was confronted with a dispute between Christians. One group claimed that believers should abstain from eating meat that had been offered to idols and then sold on the market. The meat was perfectly safe for human consumption, but it was spiritually contaminated, they said, and thus should be avoided. The other group thought this was silly. The meat was fine. Good food is a gift from God and should be eaten with gratitude.

Paul could have taken the easy route and used his authority to declare the meat to be either clean or unclean and put an end to the issue right there, but he didn't. Instead, he opened up a can of worms by saying that if the meat offends you, leave it alone. If it doesn't, then eat it. "Each of them should be fully convinced in their own mind" (Rom. 14:5).

This is the classic "let your conscience be your guide," but with a major twist. A conscience that's saturated in truth is the only conscience that can be trusted. Furthermore, Paul says we should keep these things between us and God, because no one else has the right to judge us or tell us exactly how to think. He does, however, raise the bar for those who are convinced they have the freedom to eat the meat by challenging them *not* to eat it, if it will cause a "weaker" brother to stumble. Everything God created is for us to enjoy, but leave it to evil influences to take the good things we were intended to enjoy and twist them into trouble and confusion.

When God's spirit speaks into a life and begins placing before that person a higher calling—like my friend experienced when God spoke to her about her sex life—He always has a higher purpose in mind. A life deeply marked by self-control doesn't gain our acceptance by God; He already loves us. Jesus' sacrifice was all about that. But self-control does help us keep the effects of sin out of our lives and gives us the opportunity to be ready for the next step in God's plan. Ultimately, self-control creates a confident and proven faith that invites Him to work more effectively through our lives . . . a concept that those who lack spiritual discernment absolutely do not get.

Choosing to do the right thing in a difficult moment will require us to trust God's promises of strength and wisdom, not in a mystical way but in a very practical way. The apostle Paul was extremely practical when he reminded us that God will never allow us to be tempted beyond what we can bear, but instead will provide a way out so that we can stand up under it: "No temptation has overtaken you except what is common to mankind. And God is faithful; he will not let you be tempted beyond what you can bear. But when you are tempted, he will also provide a way out so that you can endure it" (1 Cor. 10:13). This means that before we intentionally commit any sin or make any bad choice, there will always be a moment of clarity presented to us and an escape clause, if we're looking for it. God will hear our cry and give us exactly what we need to be victorious in any situation—the back door escape—and then reward us for a job well done.

This was an early spiritual lesson in the "give and take" of self-control for my college friend. God had plans for her that required a choice to be set apart. She chose to do the right thing, and God not only supplied her with everything she needed with regard to her boyfriend that fateful night, He also strengthened her faith which prepared her for the plans that lay ahead. He also threw in a really good marriage to the boy whose night ended so abruptly, and so painfully, many years ago. They've been married thirty years.

Spiritual Attack

If sin is not the direct cause of spiritual doubt, then spiritual attack may be. Theologians often refer to this attack as "spiritual warfare," but whatever the forces of evil look like or whatever form the "evil one" takes, very early in our Christian training we learn that he doesn't care half as much about how we look on Sunday morning as he does about what we're up to the rest of the week.

Spiritual warfare, for lack of a better definition, is the cosmic outworking of the battle between good and evil. Again, resisting caricatures, it isn't about Stephen King novels, beds that levitate or walls that drip blood. It's much more subtle than that and far more deadly— appealing to our senses like the attractive coworker who gives us attention and assures us that our husband could never appreciate us the way he should. Or like the expense account that if just barely altered could provide desperate financial relief. Who would know?

If we actually saw evil as it's portrayed in horror movies, we'd steer clear. Problem solved. But even the New Testament describes the "evil one" as masquerading as an "angel of light." He makes it look good, sound good, and feel good even when it leads to destruction. When we willingly submit to what we know to be wrong, we lower our guard and become vulnerable to his continued attack. We also put a confident faith at risk. Conversely, nothing builds confidence faster than doing everything possible to make the right decision.

The mysterious tension between good and evil is a consequence to man's full autonomy. Anything less would threaten our freedom of choice. And though Christians are more comfortable saying that God didn't create evil, they would at the very least need to concede that He created the potential, and that in doing so, He displayed a disinterest in creating a race of robotic humanoids.

We see evidence of God making use of the tension between good and evil to achieve His purposes regularly, but the most striking example of this is found in the familiar narrative of the Old Testament character whose name has become synonymous with suffering. The story of Job was meant to illustrate the cosmic battle by pointing out the fact that Job didn't do anything wrong. He wasn't being punished for his sin. Instead, God gave Satan permission to test Job with six little words that haunt us; "Have you considered my servant Job?" (Job 1:8). You'll notice that Job never found out why he suffered and you'll also notice that he pelted God with some rather big questions—otherwise known as doubt. Ultimately, spiritual doubt is the fallout of spiritual warfare—the residuals of the battles that are waged in and over our lives.

A word of caution here. Most of us tend toward the extreme when we consider the concept of evil: some adamantly deny its existence, blaming all objectionable behavior on faulty genes or questionable upbringing, and others become preoccupied with it, looking for it, and thus finding it, everywhere. But when it comes to evil, we need to guard against extremes because denying its existence leaves us vulnerable to its wiles, and obsessing over it turns us into fanatic nuts.

We need to strike the proper balance because while spiritual warfare may originate in the "heavenly realms," as Ephesians 6 points out, its battles wage on earth in a profoundly practical and personal way. Caring little about whether or not we believe, as C. S. Lewis points out in *Screwtape Letters*, somehow the enemy knows how to keep the battle real by finding our most vulnerable spots, then taking aim and firing: "For though we live in the world, we do not wage war as the world does. The weapons we fight with are not the weapons of the world. On the contrary, they have divine power to demolish strongholds. We demolish arguments and every pretension that sets itself up against the knowledge of God, and we take captive every thought to make it obedient to Christ" (2 Cor. 10:3–5). This all may sound a bit otherworldly, but we can be sure it is not. In fact, I find it interesting that sensationalized reports of demonic oppression tend to land on the cover of the *National Enquirer*. But it's the genuine stories of personal and global destruction that greet us every night on the evening news. These are the stories of evil personified, the genuine article. If we want to deal with the problem of evil effectively, we need to avoid the counterproductive nature of both extremes, neither overemphasizing nor underestimating it. We need to keep it real.

Spiritual doubt emerges when we willfully make bad decisions and as the powers of darkness wage their war against righteousness. The battle may originate in the heavenly realms, but its consequences are oppressively earthbound. So how do we combat spiritual doubt?

Spiritual Intimacy

Scripture uses the family unit to illustrate our relationship with God. And this makes sense, since He crafted the human metaphor for precisely that purpose. The "rules" that work in human relationships are often the same ones that shape our relationship with Him. The more time we spend talking to and listening to a loving earthly father, the more assured we are of his love, his presence, and his impact in our lives. And so it is with our "Heavenly Father." If we are angry, wounded, or frustrated, yet willing to share those concerns, the opportunity to bond, to grow closer, and even to give each other the benefit of the doubt will become evident. Returning to the basic, *uncluttered* truth of who Jesus is and how He can provide intimacy with God genuinely transforms lives and strengthens faith.

Developing intimacy with God enables us to become proactive against spiritual doubt on every level. And while spiritual intimacy may sound ethereal, or something better left to the experts, mystics, and gurus, we can be assured that it's not. This kind of spiritual intimacy flows from the spiritual disciplines of prayer and meditation on God's truth. It equips us with the armor of God described in Ephesians 6. We're not talking about Eastern mysticism where we clear our minds, assume the lotus position, and chant. It's a rubber-meets-the-road, down and dirty kind of thing. It's wrestling with God just like Jacob did in the Bible narrative, where it was physically rough enough that Jacob was left with a permanent limp.

The prospect of spiritual intimacy is extremely practical for *everyone*, which is precisely why I share my college story. Too often leaders and teachers leave the impression that they are somehow above sin and temptation, but I'd be uncomfortable if people believed that of me or if they thought I believed that of myself. There is no room for hypocrisy in God's plans. Jesus saw to that. I still remember the surprise on my husband's young Catholic face when we both realized that the Bible teaches that *all* have sinned and fall short of God's perfection. That includes everyone, even the Pope or Billy Graham. Even Mary, the mother of Jesus, as amazing as she was, needed a Savior and referred to God as hers, in Luke chapter 1. We are all battling against doubt and the sin that so often causes it.

I've since logged a lot of years as a believer, and one of the things I'm convinced of is that following Christ is not a mystical experience. It is intensely pragmatic. Even the miracles found in Scripture are the exception rather than the rule. Building a foundation to combat spiritual warfare should be straightforward because it's the "everyday" that causes us problems. Our routine creeps in and, much like a new romance, unless there is a foundation in place to deal effectively with the ups and downs, we will struggle.

Jesus said,

> Therefore whoever hears these sayings of Mine, and does them, I will liken him to a wise man who built his house on the rock: and the rain descended, the floods came, and the winds blew and beat on that house; and it did not fall, for it was founded on the rock.
>
> But everyone who hears these sayings of Mine, and does not do them, will be like a foolish man who built his house on the sand: and the rain descended, the floods came, and the winds

blew and beat on that house; and it fell. And great was its fall.
(Matt. 7:24–27 NKJV)

Contrary to what televangelists on fringe cable channels might indicate as they urge us to send money, God isn't looking for emotionally
charged onetime events. Genuine, consistent pursuers of truth are less
concerned about orchestrated momentary *decisions* and far more concerned about genuine growth and *discipleship*. It isn't about coercion
or manipulation; it's about living out the truth. God's Word seems to
indicate that He wants us in this life-journey with Him for the long
haul—the marathon. It's not easy, and it's not always fun, but it is profoundly rewarding.

Spiritual intimacy with God breeds a confident faith—one that
knows God cares and will do what is best because it's been proven. Some
of the most significant times of faith building in my own life have simply been the result of practical steps I've taken to overcome sin. It's not
about special rituals or potions, but simply choosing to make the right
decision and doing everything we can to make that happen, whether it
involves ending a relationship, changing a job, working with a counselor, or even seeking medical advice.

Ultimately, spiritual intimacy is about having a relationship with
God—listening to Him speak, spending time with Him in prayer and
confession, and meditating on His truths. Regardless of how we feel
about it, it's through these simple spiritual disciplines that we draw near
to God, and He draws near to us, just as He promised: "You will seek
me and find me when you seek me with all your heart (Jer. 29:13).

Looking Deeper

1. Identify sources of spiritual attack in your life.
2. What keeps you vulnerable?
3. When is sin most difficult to identify?

Chapter 4

HE SPEAKS

Stanley Tretick was a photographer for *Look* magazine and captured an amusing shot of John Jr. in 1963 as a toddler playing under the president's desk in the Oval Office. Obviously missing from the photograph are the bodyguards and secret service agents who most certainly lined the West Wing, keeping anyone other than John John out from under that desk. As the boy played, the father looked pleased to have him so close, revealing an intimacy reserved only for father and child. A very powerful man enjoying the nearness of his beloved child.

This is the imagery God uses to define our relationship with Him: Father and child. God reserves the right to determine the potential of our relationship with Him, and His desire for intimacy is revealed throughout Scripture. As I began studying all of the great religions of the world, I discovered a common thread. Clearly, they all have something of value to offer, but each one of them reflects man's attempt to reach up to God by good deeds and religious behavior. It's only in the Christian faith that we're forced to face our inability to reach God by our own efforts. That's the bad news. The good news, which is what the word "gospel" literally means, is that God reaches down to us through Christ, a plan that does not make Christians arrogant, as cynics often charge, but brings a level of confidence that is available to everyone, including the cynic. And this appears to have been God's plan for us all along, laid out for us, Scripture indicates, before the foundations of the earth (1 Peter 1:20).

It's interesting to note that people, no matter the time period or location, have attempted to get a handle on God. All things considered, the human race has done a good job of trying to comprehend something of God and His truth through nature, philosophy, the arts and sciences, and the like. Exploring, creating, and pressing toward answers is such an integral part of man's DNA, we can safely assume that, for purposes known only to Him, God has ordained our search for truth.

But whether we're considering an abstract Spinozan God or a more concrete being, the fact is we would know very little about Him personally had He not chosen to reveal Himself specifically to us first. Julian Casserley states, "The gospel provides that knowledge of ultimate truth which men have sought through philosophy in vain, inevitably in vain, because it is essential to the very nature of God that He cannot be discovered by the searching and probing of human minds, that He can only be known if He first takes the initiative and reveals Himself."[1]

It makes sense that if God invented us, He might also want to communicate with us. If we are going to dig in and become intimate with Him and stave off spiritual doubt, we obviously must begin by knowing how He desires to communicate with us. Personally, I've never heard audible voices, but over the years I've become convinced that God speaks to us in several ways. He speaks through creation and conscience. He speaks through the prophets and the apostles which led to Him speaking directly to each one of us through the Scriptures—otherwise known as the Bible. So how is it that we distinguish God's voice?

Hearing God's Voice

When my daughter was five, we were in the center of a crowded mall when I suddenly lost sight of her. She'd been by my side only seconds earlier, but I immediately began to panic. Figuring she couldn't have gone far, I let out a scream that was so loud and so primal I almost scared myself. "Alissa!"

Suddenly, like a scene from the Twilight Zone, I became the man with the stopwatch and the entire mall froze. The only movement came from a little towheaded figure stepping out from behind a kiosk. Slightly annoyed, she asked, "What?"

Relief coursed through my veins with the same intensity panic had only seconds before. Since then, I've teased her and said that had I known the challenge she'd be in her teen years, I might not have yelled quite so loudly, but what amazes me about that day, is that while scores of people heard me scream, looked my direction, and froze, only one of them answered. It was the one who recognized her mother's voice. "The sheep listen to his voice. He calls his own sheep by name and leads them out" (John 10:3). When we learn how to recognize the voice of God amidst the din of life, and we choose to respond or obey, we discover what it means to confidently keep in step with the Spirit.

Listening to God's Voice

But I've discovered that the real question isn't whether or not I understand what He might be saying to me, but whether or not I'm willing to listen. There is, after all, a huge difference between hearing and listening, though the process of listening is not as complicated as it sounds.

While Scripture tells us that God can use just about anything to speak to us—even nature and evil men—the Bible is also the only form of communication known as the Word of God.

So, naturally, the question is, if God speaks to us most clearly through His Word, why don't we spend more time reading it? Some stay away because of bad experiences they've had with it, or, more specifically, bad experiences they've had with those who've misused or abused it. Others avoid the Bible because they're too cynical to even consider the possibility that a God may have created them and initiated a connection with them. Still others say they don't read the Bible because they've already read it, as though God doesn't speak to us in a fresh way every time we open His Word.

Early in my panic disorder, I realized that I needed more than a religious experience or a philosophical perspective. I needed more than self-actualization, a mantra, or something that could be generated through my own will. I was the source of my trouble, so I knew I needed the infusion of a power that didn't originate with me—something outside myself.

In the New Testament, the apostle Paul's letter to Timothy points out the power of God's revelation to train and equip us in life: "All Scripture is God-breathed and is useful for teaching, rebuking, correcting and training in righteousness, so that the servant of God may be thoroughly equipped for every good work" (2 Tim. 3:16–17).

In the Old Testament, Psalm 119 is a virtual celebration of God's Word. Beginning in verse 97, the psalmist says, "Oh, how I love your law! I meditate on it all day long." He goes on to say that God's Word dispels darkness from the human heart, it illuminates our steps, and it tastes as sweet as honey. I've often thought, as I've read Psalm 119, that this kind of adulation and enlightenment can only come from someone who has stumbled around in the dark. The desire to think about God's Word all day and night could only come from someone who is not only desperate and confused, but likely also struggling with tough questions that elicit doubt.

Jill Briscoe has always said, "A Bible falling apart usually belongs to someone who isn't." Both Jill and the psalmist model spectacular spiritual strength because when hard times strike them, they run to Scripture—the place where they know renewal is found.

There is a powerful story tucked away in the Old Testament that illustrates this truth. It's about a young king who came into power at the tender age of eight. He inherited a kingdom of chaos from his father, who had embraced idolatry and was eventually assassinated. But by Josiah's eighteenth year, he displayed a heart for God and a desire to draw on His wisdom and strength.

Second Kings tells us that after Josiah ordered repairs on the neglected temple, during renovation, the book of the Law was uncovered. When the dust was blown off and the words of the Lord were read to the king, he tore his robe in contrition as he recognized how far from God his people had moved. Josiah's repentance brought blessing from the God who is in the restoration business, including the promise that he would one day die in peace. It's worth noting that Josiah's life and the lives of those around him were completely changed because they began reading the Scriptures again. Scripture offers clarity in the midst of our confusion by providing the guidance we need along with the guidelines for living a life that produces joy, peace, patience, and the rest of the fruits of the Spirit. He was the product of a dysfunctional parent, but the truths of Scripture were able to guide him to a place of health. And this, in turn, had an enormous impact on everyone around him.

It is important to note that misinterpretation of Scripture does occur, however. Biblical scholars typically differentiate between principles, which evolve over time and through culture, and commands or moral absolutes that are fixed. Though all of Scripture is intended to strengthen our faith and enhance our intimacy with God, we often run into trouble when we read without distinguishing the difference between principles and absolutes.

To those who've been reared in legalism, it may come as a real shock that God offers tremendous latitude in terms of the choices we make. I've come to realize that there will always be people who find narrow and confining interpretations of Scripture a comfort. They like the safe feeling they get from being hemmed in. In some ways, it is perfectly acceptable to set parameters for yourself in areas where you feel tempted. However, things get dicey when people use their personal convictions, which may have some scriptural basis, to hem others in or to prevent themselves from growing and trusting in God on their own. In fact, viewing a narrower interpretation of Scripture as an absolute is the perfect recipe for introducing spiritual doubt in a believer's life.

The danger of mistaking a principle for an absolute is another reason it is critical for every believer to be reading the Word of God for themselves. It is much more difficult for another person to sway you if you have a solid understanding of what the Bible *actually* says. Stuart Briscoe took this healthy, minimalist approach to teaching, never trying to coerce or cajole on a topic, but instead allowing God to teach each one of us personally through His Word. The essential truth of any passage can be viewed as a command only when it's able to cross cultural barriers. So when Paul talks in 1 Timothy about the modesty of women, he was taking issue with women who were preoccupied with their appearance to the detriment of their personal character; he was not speaking to specific clothing choices. And although this may take on a different flavor from culture to culture, the essence of propriety and honor is usually not too hard to determine.

In the grand scheme of things, God's plans are never thwarted by our decisions. I once heard a man say that he didn't want to be flying on a plane with a pilot whose time had come, and I wondered if he honestly thought God was unable to work out those kinds of logistics. When it comes to so many of our decisions, it may look like utter chaos at times, but God invites our diversity and is in no way threatened by it.

So don't let fear keep you away from strengthening your faith and finding the intimacy God desires to have with you. When He speaks, we need to listen. As the old King James Version puts it, "Faith cometh by hearing, and hearing by the word of God" (Rom. 10:17).

Christian Community

While Scripture is sometimes the most concrete way God speaks to us, Scripture also says that He speaks through Christian community. Unfortunately, few things seem less appealing than dealing with people when we're struggling with doubt, depression, or despair. Pain often prefers solitude, but that's something we need to resist because we need each other. That's the way God wired us. As imperfect as it is, the universal church is called the "body of Christ" for a reason. We are spiritually interconnected, and when one suffers, we all suffer. When one is restored, we are all restored. The apostle Paul uses our physical bodies to illustrate: "The eye cannot say to the hand, 'I don't need you!' And the head cannot say to the feet, 'I don't need you!'" (1 Cor. 12:21).

Some parts of our body seem to clamor for attention, while others seem to sit quietly unnoticed, but each one is important. Several years ago, on the soft beach sand of Baileys Harbor in Wisconsin, my two nieces and their boyfriends wanted to have a long-jump competition. My competitive nature immediately kicked in, probably because they were twenty and I was forty, but for whatever reason, in my zest to win, I stepped badly and immediately broke my toe. It wasn't too painful in the moment; my wounded pride deflected any awareness of that. But by the next day, the innocuous little digit, one I'd hardly noticed before, was screaming for attention as it lay slightly askew and outlined by every color of the rainbow.

Many women take the role of that innocuous, seemingly unnecessary little appendage. They sit quietly and prefer to go unnoticed. When they hurt, they are reluctant to share their pain, afraid of the unwanted attention they may receive. They may feel insignificant, but they, too, need to share their burdens, their fears, their doubts, with others. They need attention within the body. Even women in positions of church leadership are leery of confession, lest someone discover they live with an abusive spouse, an addicted teen, or a cross-dressing sibling. Who can they tell of their humiliating DUI? As a confidant, I am completely safe. I in no position to judge, and I'll be leaving on the next flight.

When did church become a place only for the shiny, happy people whose lives appear all together? I don't see any sign of that in Scripture. David Kinnaman, president of the Barna Group, has written extensively on the "image problem" that plagues Christianity in our culture today. It comes as no surprise to the younger generation that the church often appears self-righteous and completely out of touch. When they realize they can't live up to what appears to them as perfection and exclusivity, they check out and move on. And who can blame them?

Sometimes religious people set the bar so high that when others fail to measure up, they simply opt out and ask, why try?—a classic parent/child paradigm that can frustrate kids who may decide to give up because they cannot measure up. I once heard a wise pastor say, "Don't make Christianity hard for your kids." Indeed, God's holiness should take our breath away, but it's His desire to remain accessible to us in light of our "unholiness" that should leave us breathless.

To the people of Corinth, the apostle Paul refers to Jesus in a way that never ceases to amaze me: "God made him who had no sin to be sin for us, so that in him we might become the righteousness of God" (2 Cor. 5:21). Our sin and evil was not ignored, nor was it denied. It was dealt with in a big way.

The truth is, all around me I see people whose pain has threatened their faith and left them thinking they are beyond fixing. Yet Jesus entered humanity precisely for them, not for the so-called perfect people. "It is not the healthy who need a doctor, but the sick. . . . For I have not come to call the righteous, but sinners" (Matt. 9:12–13).

Jesus' words should be a wake-up call for churches everywhere. Many, though clearly not all of them, may need to ask themselves, if we cannot be honest, approachable, and ready to invest in someone else's problems, why are we doing the "church thing" to begin with? Little wonder so many people, even those who profess strong spiritual convictions, stay away. There are no promises of perfection this side of heaven, only a call for a shared burden and an unconditional love that can come very close.

I'm an outdoor runner, and it's tough to supplement my workouts on a treadmill. Nothing short of golf-sized hail can confine me to the mundane task. On one such day, while channel surfing, I landed on CNN where Prince Charles was preparing to deliver a speech. I watched him walk onto the stage and take the microphone while a marching band sat quietly behind him. Suddenly, a young man flailing a handgun leapt onto the stage and headed toward him. The gunman was immediately tackled by the secret servicemen who'd been standing guard, and the entire episode was over in less than thirty seconds. The media, however, continued to buzz.

One cameraman in particular caught my attention as the drama unfolded. I noticed that in his pursuit of the perfect shot he was backing up, too focused to check where he was stepping. He seemed unaware of the fact that he was inching ever closer to the edge of the stage. I stopped my running for a second and waited to see the poor guy take the plunge. Just then, as he was about to reach the point of no return, another man who was also wired up in headgear came up from behind him and placed his hands on the filming man's waist. He gently guided him to safer footing, which allowed the cameraman to keep filming without looking away for even a second. He never missed a shot.

The scene played out like poetry in motion, but what struck me was the fact that those two guys had no idea what was going to happen that morning when they grabbed their coffee and headed to work. Yet, because of their commitment, the two functioned as one and successfully accomplished the common goal.

This is exactly how the church, the body of Christ, was meant to function. We're called to be each other's eyes, each other's hands, and each other's feet. We're called to invest in each other's pain, bind up each other's wounds, and share each other's burdens without a hint of the caustic judgmentalism we're so often accused of. Connecting with people who have our backs—to both protect us and gently prompt redirection—provides a kind of strength that lends itself to spiritual confidence.

Looking Deeper

1. When does God's voice sound clearest to you?
2. When has it seemed that God was silent when you needed Him to speak?
3. What makes it difficult to hear from God?

Chapter 5

HE LISTENS

Equally important to hearing from God is speaking to Him. Another way to combat spiritual doubt and strengthen our intimacy with God is through prayer and meditation. From the beginning of time, long before God initiated what we would call a formal religious system through Abraham, humans have put a premium on getting God's attention. This is no surprise anthropologically speaking. It's even less of a surprise scripturally speaking. "From one man he made all the nations, that they should inhabit the whole earth; and he marked out their appointed times in history and the boundaries of their lands. God did this so that they would seek him and perhaps reach out for him and find him, though he is not far from any one of us" (Acts 17:26–27). God not only allows us to come to Him in prayer but instructs us to.

When I was a kid, I hated camp. I was miserably homesick and clearly every camp counselor's nightmare. I battled insomnia at night and greeted nausea by day. On the other hand, my older sister, who was also at camp, wrote letters home that were filled with glowing reviews of swimming, horseback riding, and campfires. It was hard to believe we had attended the same camp when my words home were more like, "Why hast thou forsaken me?" My parents held onto the letters for years. Scrawled on the bottom of one of my sister's letters was simply, "Come and get Ann."

It was brutal, and the irony of visiting so many camps across the country now as a speaker is never lost on me. But summer camp does hold one bright memory that involves the bunkhouse leader I was assigned to who obviously drew the short straw. We all loved her. Not only was she beautiful, with long flowing brown hair, but we knew she was brilliant too. She knew *everything*. She was seventeen.

Her name escapes me now, but she is personally responsible for teaching me what it means to take seriously the charge found in 1 Thessalonians 5:17 to "pray continually." One evening, as we sat in a circle on the bunkhouse floor, she explained, "When I wake up in the morning, before I even step out of bed, I greet the Lord in prayer. Throughout the day, I share the concerns I have and all the things I have to be thankful for. But I never say *amen* until I get back in bed at night."

Traumatized or not, this insight has never left me. I apply it to my life every day because I'm convinced that as mysterious as prayer is, it is not only a privilege but a powerful resource. Through prayer we receive strength, guidance, and peace from God. We are transformed. What Scripture doesn't tell us, however, is how prayer works, and for some people this is a major stumbling block and a source of tremendous spiritual doubt. We tend to distance ourselves from things we don't understand. Why should we ask God for what He already knows we need (see Matt. 6:8)? What difference will it make if He is already working out everything in conformity to the purpose of His will (see Eph. 1:11)?

When my grandma died, I was invited to help myself to the books she left on her shelf. To this day, every time I open her copy of *Knowing God* by J. I. Packer and see the notes she scribbled, I feel as though I'm standing on holy ground. Another book that caught my attention as I scoured her shelf was put together by an apologist who answered people's toughest Bible questions on Moody Radio many years ago. I grabbed it and immediately looked up *prayer* in the index to see if he would speculate on how it works.

He first pointed out the fact that God doesn't change (Mal. 3:6).

Then, acknowledging his belief that God's sovereign plans were worked out before the creation of time, he admitted that to us, humanly speaking, our prayers might seem like a waste of time. However, the good Calvinist in him didn't stop there. Instead, he went on to speculate that God never has to change His plans based on us. From the beginning, he explained, God knew exactly how each one of us would react in every situation and exactly how we would pray. Thus, He made His plans accordingly.

I found his concepts intriguing, but reasoned that if a mere man could come up with something that coherent, certainly God could come up with an explanation that was even better. He's not limited to our wildest imaginings. As Paul said in Ephesians 3, God is able to do the immeasurable, more than any of us could think of or ask for, which for some of us is quite a bit.

Simply put, prayer is a personal conversation with God. He invites us to enter into His presence—a place where His hand mysteriously moves and we are changed—and this is a gift beyond measure. Jesus taught us to pray in His name (John 14:13–14) and for His will (Matt. 6:10), and when we do, our perceptions become enlarged, our emotions centered, and our spiritual doubts less invasive.

In the Old Testament book of Jeremiah, the Lord says, "Call to me and I will answer you and tell you great and unsearchable things you do not know" (33:3).

One of the more common objections atheists and agnostics have to the idea of a personal God is that if there were a higher power vast enough to create the universe, it would have far better things to do than be interested in the details of our insignificant lives. Satirist Bill Maher has gone so far as to say that even if there were an Almighty Being, Christians are completely egocentric to think He wouldn't have better things to do than care about their puny needs.

Actually, having said this, Maher finds himself in good company. While considering the cosmos, King David asked the same question:

"When I consider your heavens, the work of your fingers, the moon and the stars, which you have set in place, what is mankind that you are mindful of them, human beings that you care for them?" (Ps. 8:3–4). Comparatively speaking, we are quite small, and were God not to initiate some sort of communication with us, we'd be left to our own devices trying to read nature, interpret circumstances, and get His attention.

Periodically, I like to treat myself to a physics lesson online. The beauty of YouTube is that someone like me, who focused more on cheerleading than studying in school, is able to make up for lost time. I press *pause* to look up unfamiliar terms and replay sentences until they make sense. And I can do all this without interrupting the professor or annoying the class. Some find it challenging to strike the balance between faith and science, but why should there ever be a conflict? To make a scientific discovery is to learn more about the creative forces of God.

Lawrence Krauss is a passionate antitheist who seems to think there is a conflict between science and God. In what he confessed to be a rare moment of humility, he admitted that there is much about the universe we don't know. The wonder of science is that there's still so much left to learn and discover which is why he loves being a scientist. But, Krauss says, to stop exploring and asking questions and to be satisfied by simply saying God did it would be intellectually lazy, and I agree. Far more significantly, every theistic scientist I've ever studied would agree. The Bible is not a science book. It was never intended to be. It is a spiritual book; a revelation of God.

My comfort zone is in words, which is precisely why I'm fascinated by those who have mastered numbers. Renowned theoretical physicist Michio Kaku is one of those people. In a lecture Dr. Kaku gave on quantum mechanics, he spoke of the profound mystery of black holes. With regard to the mystery, scientists use the term *singularity* to describe the infinite number of zeroes they consistently come up with when they take two proven math equations, both pertaining to quantum physics, and try to reconcile them with one another. The task is impossible, the calculations, unanswerable, Kaku said. A virtual nightmare for the physicist, another said. An embarrassment, as scientists are never comfortable with something they can't get a handle on.

As I listened to the brilliant men talking about the "astronomically heavy and infinitesimally small" holes, how they seem to collapse everything we know about the physical universe, and what could possibly come out of them, I thought about what a great sci-fi novel that would make. Then I thought about the story of the Tower of Babel in the book of Genesis. Whether one takes it literally or not, the message is clear: Man's attempt to reach God or stand on His level is futile, as futile as our efforts to grasp infinity.

When we try to understand the vastness of God and how insignificant man is comparatively speaking, we're able to appreciate the profound privilege of prayer. In a Barbara Walters interview years ago, Barbara did what she does best and brought Goldie Hawn to tears. Goldie told a touching story about how her father taught her to keep our little lives in perspective. If ever she was tempted to feel too big, he told her to stand on the beach and look out over the massive ocean.

When I pray, I often feel like King David did. I don't want to be selfish or bother God with my seemingly insignificant problems. Most of us would have to admit that many of our concerns seem microscopic in the scheme of life's bigger tragedies. Still, I've processed just enough life to be convinced that a mother's pain is a mother's pain, whether it's rooted in a Haitian struggle to find food for a hungry child or living in Western plenty yet watching one's offspring slowly destroyed by rejection and self-loathing. And the Scriptures teach us that like any empathetic parent, if our concerns are significant to us, they are significant to Him, and we should bring all of them to Him in prayer (1 Peter 5:7). God could have chosen to remain aloof or anonymous. He holds that prerogative, and those of us who know Him understand that very well.

But He didn't choose to stay removed. Instead, He decided to engage us in relationship, intimacy, and even conversation. In fact, He uses the entire human race to illustrate His desire for intimacy. Even in the most dysfunctional settings, most of us have an innate sense of what a good father should look like. God instituted the family unit—a concept that crosses virtually every cultural constraint—showed us what a father is, and then invited us to call Him Abba Father.

Through the practice of prayer and meditation on truth, God's Spirit meets with us on an intimate level, where He not only comforts us and speaks to our doubts but directs us as well. Prayer is the place where we can bring our desperation, our fears, our requests, all of who we are and hope to be and then, like the psalmist, find our doubt falling away in favor of praising Him for His interaction in our lives.

Putting It to Use

Years ago, I was booked to speak at a women's conference in Toronto. It was my first assignment as an international speaker, but my excitement was short-lived. A few weeks before I was to travel north, I got a call from the coordinator asking if after my event on Saturday I'd consider speaking at a large Sunday morning church service in the area.

I agreed to her offer and was initially fine with the idea, but after I hung up the phone I began to wonder if I'd made a mistake. Up to that point, I'd only spoken to women at women's events. This, however, was a Sunday morning church service and would definitely include a mixed crowd. I wasn't sure how I felt about talking to men and suddenly remembered the horror stories Jill Briscoe had told me about some of her unpleasant experiences. One involved several men who'd yelled their objections to her as she began to speak. Another involved a bunch of seminary boys who sat quietly in the front row as she made her way to the platform. They were fine with her introductions, but as soon as she began to teach, they stood up in unison and walked out in protest.

I had just come off a thirteen-year battle with panic attacks, and I wasn't looking for trouble. I was no Rosa Parks. It was not my intention to break ground among disapproving men. Speaking from experience, Jill offered a few thoughts, mentioned several books, and suggested I spend some time in prayer.

I began my quest for direction by looking at the apostle Paul's instructions to the church in Corinth. Addressing a problem of disorder, he said, "Women should remain silent in the churches" (1 Cor. 14:34). Traditionally, these passages have been interpreted in one of two ways: from a *prescriptive* manner, prescribing how things *should be*, or from a *descriptive* manner, describing how things *have become*.

However, the more Scripture and commentary I read, the more confusing it seemed. Turns out that Christians, even ones with the best of intentions, have been divided on this issue for a very long time. For example, Catherine Booth, cofounder of the Salvation Army, recognized the importance of women and their God-given duty to serve Him wherever and whenever they're needed. This includes preaching.

After reading her inspiring words I was ready to sign up and probably should have stopped there. But I didn't and quickly discovered polar opposite opinions, including that of evangelist Dr. John R. Rice, who wrote *Bobbed Hair, Bossy Wives and Women Preachers.* The title is a dead giveaway.

Not mincing words, Dr. Rice was convinced that millions of people will "go to hell" because of the unscriptural practices of women preachers. That wasn't too reassuring, so I decided to go back further into church history and look at what some of the early church fathers had to say. Perhaps Augustine, Origen, or Tertullian could bring some clarity to this convoluted topic. And, in a strange way, they did.

Some of their ideas were clearly based on Scripture, but others seemed more like what we might call sanctified hunches. Two of the more entertaining perspectives I gleaned from Ruth Tucker's research, and they went something like this: *Women should teach the truth in love, but men should not sit and listen. Nature indicates that women were not meant to stand up and preach. Their hips are wider and their shoulders are narrower, proving they were created to sit and listen.*

By the time I finished reading, I should have been more confused than when I started, but I wasn't. Because I had continued to pray for God's direction through it all, a slow steady confidence was starting to take root. I knew God wasn't playing some sadistic guessing game with me, just waiting for me to mess up. He knew my heart. He also knew that as much as I didn't want to be found standing up if I should be sitting down, I didn't want to be found sitting down if I should be standing up. So I stood, and we were all blessed.

The truth is, my nature is such that it would never allow me to take a risk if I couldn't bank on God's grace. In fact, whenever I pray about things that weigh heavily on me and receive peace, it really does move me beyond all understanding. My neurotic tendencies steer me away from peace, and my propensity for melancholy and skepticism would never generate faith in God. Thus, there is only one explanation: "The Spirit Himself bears witness with our spirit" (Rom. 8:16 NKJV).

I know that through prayer and meditation I will have every opportunity to make the right decision and find peace. But even if I get it wrong, I still have confidence that if my motives are right, God will see my intensions and give the grace needed to cover my mistakes.

Confession

And we do make mistakes. We become wounded too. Sometimes our pain and doubt are so severe that we're too wounded to even pray. But, incredibly, God makes provision for that too. When our words have dried up, the apostle Paul says we have an advocate we can count on who will step in on our behalf: "Jesus Christ . . . is at the right hand of God and is also interceding for us" (Rom. 8:34).

Most importantly, Scripture teaches that our relationship with God is protected by God Himself and is secure because of that protection. Eternal life is called *eternal* for a reason. It doesn't end. Jesus said in

John 5:24 that believers have crossed over (past tense) from death to life. We are sealed by the Holy Spirit, which brings to mind the picture of an envelope sealed by the wax imprint of a king's ring.

Because our relationship with Christ is not predicated on our behavior, it isn't jeopardized by what we do—past, present, or future—either. Rather, it is based solely on what He has done for us. When we have a fight with our spouse, it doesn't make us any less married—though for a moment we may wish it did—but it isn't until someone chokes out the words, "I'm sorry," that genuine intimacy can be restored. So it is with God: "If we confess our sins, he is faithful and just and will forgive us our sins" (1 John 1:9).

Sinning won't end our relationship with God, but it will impact our intimacy with Him, just as it would with anyone we have a strong disagreement with. David said, "If I had cherished sin in my heart, the Lord would not have listened" (Ps. 66:18). It's not as though an omniscient God couldn't hear David's words; it's about how God would have responded. Sin lays the groundwork for spiritual doubt to take root, not only by threatening our confidence in God but also by threatening our confidence in ourselves. Whether we are aware of it or not, guilt has the power to keep us trapped in the solitude of self-loathing.

The interesting thing is that God can use our spiritual doubt to create *more* intimacy with him. It brings with it a great opportunity for us to examine ourselves and see where we are before God. A friend, a pastor, or a counselor can often see areas of our lives that are derailing before we can. They can offer objective advice that can guide us toward the kind of clear thinking that will combat doubt. Have we neglected the intimacy God offers us through Christ, through His Word, and through prayer? Have we decided His plans aren't clever or modern enough for us? He has given us an arsenal to combat evil and become victorious in our spiritual lives. Perhaps it's time we pick up the weapons of Scripture, community, prayer and meditation, and confession and do battle against the doubt caused by sin and spiritual attack.

Looking Deeper

1.   How do you best communicate with God?
2.   Identify an obstacle to your own spiritual growth.
3.   What would you be willing to do to overcome that obstacle?

Chapter 6

INTELLECTUAL DOUBT

Sometimes doubts are spiritual, but other times they are purely intellectual—good questions demanding practical answers. And, for the record, we should definitely be asking more questions than we do. However, many of us avoid asking the big ones for a number of reasons. Some of us were taught that our inquiries are a sign of disrespect or unbelief. Others of us are afraid our faith will buckle under pressure. Some sidestep investigations altogether, fearing that God will somehow be offended. But if God is really God, how could He ever be threatened by us? If our faith is rooted in truth and our ability to reason is a gift from Him, shouldn't He be able to handle any question we could come up with?

In Scripture, believers are instructed to aggressively pursue all sides of faith: spiritual, intellectual, and emotional. In Deuteronomy 6:5, Moses instructs the children of Israel to love the Lord their God with their hearts, their souls, and their strength. In Matthew 22:37, Matthew splits the atom even further when Jesus adds that we are to love the Lord our God with our *minds* as well. No excuse for checking your brain at the door of the church here. It's interesting to me that the most popular teaching technique in the Jewish culture is the practice of asking insightful questions. Over and over, Scripture indicates that we should pursue knowledge, even when that pursuit involves questions.

I recently heard a woman tell about her husband, a minister, who had run off with another woman. His self-absorbed choice to fulfill his own desires with complete disregard for his family left their eighteen-year-old son reeling. Crushed by his father's actions, he was moved to make the bold announcement that he was now an atheist.

In the movie *The Pianist,* a Jewish man whose life had been destroyed by the Nazi occupation of Poland in 1939 stood in the ghetto and made the same kind of statement: "I no longer believe in God."

If neither of these statements is difficult for us to understand, given the circumstances surrounding them, why would they be difficult for God to understand? Life is filled with similar discord on both a personal and a global scale. Suffering people often feel God has let them down, a concept that's often too painful or shameful to even admit. So, in order to come to terms with the idea that God would allow such suffering, they try to minimize His involvement or minimize Him.

Rabbi Kushner did this in his book *When Bad Things Happen to Good People.* In light of his own difficult experiences, he felt that the concept of an all-powerful and all-loving God was incongruous. His pain dictated that God is either short on love or limited in His power. Kushner chose the latter.

When Bad Is Good

The suffering we see in the world can be a major stumbling block to faith, but what may be even more surprising is how a severe trial can draw a person closer to God. I visited with a woman after a conference who told me her story which was a striking example of adversity bringing you closer to God. Her alcoholic father was the abuser. Her mother, though not directly involved, could be seen as equally culpable, having enabled him by turning a blind eye.

She told me that as a young girl he took her to the sleazy bar he frequented with his drunken friends who often abused her as well. The memories lingered, she said, as the mere scent of alcohol was still able to thrust her back to the nightmare. She went on to say that by the time she left home, she was a mess. I could only imagine. The most significant relationship in a child's life is with their parents. Yet, there she sat beside me, the picture of wholeness and serving in a thriving ministry to the homeless. I asked how this could be.

She told me that one day she ran into several Christians who were like no one she'd ever met. They were as imperfect as anyone else walking the planet, but they were forgiven, and they were joyful because of it. As they embraced her with open arms, she realized that the things she had done weren't important to them. Her life of drugs and promiscuity, an obvious response to her past, didn't seem to matter. They loved her, and better still, they explained that God loved her. He loved her so much, in fact, that He sent His Son to take on the entire mess.

I listened to her story, and if I was amazed up to that point, I was blown away by what she said next. Years later, after she had gotten herself together, she initiated a relationship with her father. She confronted him for the sins he had committed against her but balanced that with the grace of God, who doesn't overlook evil but offers to bridge the gap it has wedged between us. Before his death, her father confessed his sin and received forgiveness both from her and from the Lord.

In that moment, as my mentor puts it, "I saw the Pharisee in me" and was reminded of my own limitations when it comes to grace and forgiveness. Regardless of the sincerity of his confession, surely there had to be some sort of hell set aside just for him. The Bible is full of stories like this, of broken people finding the salve of relationship with Jesus. But the examples aren't just in the Bible. My friend is just one of myriad Christians who have made the conscious choice to use their horrific circumstances to become closer to their God.

Suffering introduces us to all sorts of damaged emotions—fear, disillusionment, bitterness, and even resentment. It's not easy to see others thrive when we're struggling. There may be some part of us that accepts that in God's economy it's pain that enables us to define pleasure or that it's hate that allows us to appreciate love. But when we're hurting, the beauty of this balance is lost on us. And though our emotional responses can lead to some important intellectual questions, sometimes God offers no explanations about how unfair the details of our life can seem—only the promise that He will strengthen us as He walks us through it and sort it all out at the end of the day. However, if we're left with the nagging suspicion that we might be able to do things a bit more fairly than He, we might do well to examine our hearts and pray for perspective, like Asaph did.

In Psalm 73, Asaph, one of King David's musicians, had a problem with the way God was doing things. He saw God lavishing His blessings on people who, quite frankly, didn't deserve them. He, on the other hand, who always tried to do the right thing, was going without: "But as for me, my feet had almost slipped; I had nearly lost my foothold. For I envied the arrogant when I saw the prosperity of the wicked. . . . Surely in vain I have kept my heart pure and have washed my hands in innocence. All day long I have been afflicted, and every morning brings new punishments" (vv. 2–3, 13–14).

Asaph described himself as a brute beast, with a heart that was grieved and a spirit embittered, as he poured out all his misery in that psalm. And at least two things are worth noting. First, God didn't punish him for his doubts, and second, the way Asaph felt didn't change one truth about God or His nature. In fact, the only relief Asaph found was when he forced himself to again enter the presence of God (a monumental task when we're struggling with doubt and angry with Him): "When I tried to understand all this, it troubled me deeply till I entered the sanctuary of God" (vv. 16–17). Asaph needed reminding of what doubt makes us forget: God is good, God is just, and God will meet us at the point of our greatest personal need.

It's not uncommon to hear people talk about how in the midst of their deepest trials they've found comfort in the Psalms. *Good for them*, I've always thought, hoping I'd never need them that way. But as I navigated my way through depression, finding little relief elsewhere, I picked up my Bible, kicking and screaming, and turned to the Psalms where I too found tremendous solace. Pain almost too difficult to put into words seemed to bleed from the pages:

> How long, LORD? Will you forget me forever?
>> How long will you hide your face from me?
> How long must I wrestle with my thoughts
>> and day after day have sorrow in my heart?
> How long will my enemy triumph over me?
>
> Look on me and answer, LORD my God.
>> Give light to my eyes, or I will sleep in death,
> and my enemy will say, "I have overcome him,"
>> and my foes will rejoice when I fall.
>
> But I trust in your unfailing love;
>> my heart rejoices in your salvation.
> I will sing the LORD's praise,
>> for he has been good to me. (Psalm 13)

It's as if David knew he needed to remind himself that God has been faithful and will be faithful again. His intellect understood what his painful emotions wanted him to forget. Asaph hit the nail on the head as he described how we lose sight of God's goodness and power when we hurt. His words washed over me like a soothing balm.

> I cried out to God for help;
>> I cried out to God to hear me.
> When I was in distress, I sought the Lord;
>> at night I stretched out untiring hands,
>> and I would not be comforted. . . .

My heart meditated and my spirit asked:

"Will the Lord reject forever?
    Will he never show his favor again?" . . .

Then I thought . . .
"I will remember the deeds of the LORD;
    yes, I will remember your miracles of long ago.
I will consider all your works
    and meditate on all your mighty deeds." (Ps. 77:1–2, 6–7,
10–12)

God's Response to Our Honest Questions

Even after Job filled many chapters with complaints in the book that bears his name, God never did give him an answer for why he suffered. He didn't punish Job for inquiring either. Instead, God placed His finger on the pulse of Job's pain and broadened his vision by asking, "Where were you when I laid the earth's foundation?" (Job 38:4). In God's response, He not only affirmed His power and uncompromising nature, but He also showed Job His great compassion and ultimate healing: "The LORD blessed the latter part of Job's life more than the former part" (Job 42:12).

Some questions will remain unanswered in the vastness of God, and as our vision of Him expands, so too will our ability to rest in His mysteries. Other questions will be answered when a heart honestly seeks His truth. God knows how to strike the balance by giving enough answers to remind us He is worth trusting, but retaining enough mystery to remind us He is God and we are not. Strengthening our faith in the good times is how we prepare ourselves for the bad. That's why we're instructed to be ready both "in season and out" (2 Tim. 4:2). We're to be ready to give a reason for the hope we have (1 Peter 3:15). Part of that readiness will include equipping ourselves with logical answers to questions about our faith when it comes under attack. Every Christian should be able to give reasonable answers to at least three: Is there a God? Is Jesus God? Is the Bible God's Word?

Looking Deeper

1. When have logic and faith collided in your life?
2. What impact did that have on you as a believer?
3. What's the best way to handle that conflict?

Chapter 7

IS THERE A GOD?

As a child, I believed my parents to be sensible and reliable. They proved themselves trustworthy, so when they told me about God, naturally I believed them, both because I trusted them and because what they said made sense. It was reasonable. It didn't take the intellectual arguments of Aquinas to convince me that there must be an "unmoved mover" or an "uncaused cause." Even at six, common sense dictated what the centuries-old philosopher and theologian argued: we had to have come from somewhere. And it wasn't hard for my young mind to take the logical next step. Of course, the One who made me would want me to know something of Him. Why wouldn't He?

A brief course in classical philosophy reveals plenty of intellectual giants who through the centuries have lent their unique voices to the argument for the existence of God. One of the more prominent voices of the thirteenth century was an Italian monk named Thomas Aquinas, who developed the branch of classical reasoning known as natural theology. Aquinas lived in a multicultural section of Europe rich with people who spoke different languages and engaged in different beliefs. Some believed in God; others did not, and for those who were not Christians, the Bible was nothing more than religious scribbling that Christians held dear. Unable, then, to use Scripture as a proof text, Aquinas realized that to reach others with his faith, he needed to come up with an argument for the existence of God that argued from outside the Bible.

Among Aquinas's classic arguments was the *cosmological argument* that focuses on the basic, time-tested rule of cause and effect. Something always causes something else, and because logically there cannot be an infinite regression of causes, Aquinas argued that there must be an "uncaused cause" or an "unmoved mover" that stands alone, unaffected by the constraints of time or space. We call Him God.

The *teleological argument* focuses on the orderliness and purposefulness of the universe. It argues that if someone came upon a watch lying on the ground and found it keeping perfect time, one would automatically assume someone made it. Why would the intricacies of the universe, the reproductive system, and the human circulatory system not also cry out with evidence of a maker?

Having a basic "proof" of God can become a launching pad to cement faith and deter doubt. But, again, we need to ask ourselves why we struggle with our belief in Him in the first place. Is our doubt reasonable? Those who militantly oppose the idea of any creator must allow themselves to be intellectually satisfied with nothing, except the concept that eternity-past initiated all of existence. In doing so, they must also deftly sidestep eternity's energy source, which they could just as easily refer to as God. This is precisely what David Berlinski points out in his fascinating book, *The Devil's Delusion*. The self-described skeptic and mathematician claims that new atheism is less about science and much more about ideology. Professor James Spiegel makes the same point in his book, *The Making of an Atheist*, stating that many do not want the possibility of a higher power for personal reasons, not the least of which is freedom from accountability.

Seventeenth-century philosopher, mathematician, and physicist Blaise Pascal contributed his arguments for the existence of God. Like Aquinas, he was brilliant, tinkering in his teens with what would one day become a prototype to the modern calculator. In what has come to be known as the Pascalian Wager, Pascal presented a logical argument for the existence of God that gives every doubter something to sink his teeth into. His wager, one on which I have placed my own bets a time or two, examines the probability of God's existence and ultimately explains why believing in Him is a good bet: If we believe in God and enjoy the benefits of walking with Him in this life, then get to the end of our lives and find that He does not exist and there is nothing that follows this life, we will have lost nothing. In fact, we will have gained the blessings of living with hope as a believer. If we do not believe in God and do not enjoy the benefits of life as a believer here and now, then get to the end of our lives and find Him ready to judge our arrogant unbelief, we will have lost everything. If we enjoy the benefits of being a believer now and get to the end of our lives to find that He does exist and heaven is waiting for us, we will have gained everything.

The Afterlife

With all this talk of hanging out in heaven with God, we inevitably have to ask the question, "Is there life after death?" One of the outspoken members of the New Atheists is the late Christopher Hitchens. He was an intellect with a biting humor and a style that was always entertaining. He was interviewed by Anderson Cooper on CNN and was asked about the aggressive esophageal cancer that ultimately would take his life. Hitchens conceded that a lifetime of hard drinking and smoking most certainly contributed to his disease, recognizing it would most likely take his life. But he stopped short of admitting the possibility that in death he would stand before God. Anderson smiled as he looked at Hitchens, the man's hair thinning in the final stages of cancer. But Anderson's discomfort was obvious. He then asked Hitchens what anyone watching the interview would have wanted to know at that point: "Wouldn't you want to at least hedge your bets?" Hitchens's response, at least in that moment, was no.

Anderson Cooper's conversation brings up a good point with regard to our belief in God. I don't know exactly what awaits us after this life in terms of heaven and hell. Again, there is nothing wrong with speculating, but trying to nail down too many specifics exposes a need to control what only God knows. I do know that I've wanted to live my "here and now" with God, and I want to live my "there and then" with Him as well—whatever that might look like. Volumes are written on the topic of heaven, but Scripture says precious little about what it will actually be like. However, I disagree strongly with skeptics such as Stephen Hawking who say heaven is a fairy tale invented by people who are afraid of the dark . . . and ultimately death.

The less cerebral but equally visible Brad Pitt echoes Hawking's sentiment in a 2011 interview in *The Guardian*, promoting his movie *The Tree of Life*. Pitt describes the movie's writer and director, the intensely private Terrence Malick, as a Rhodes Scholar who studied philosophy and has a love of science, nature, and God. Pitt, however, who describes his own upbringing as oppressive in the clutches of the Bible Belt, admits to almost choking on stringing those words together.

> Terry and I, we have our areas where we meet, and we have our respectful disagreements. He sees God in science and science in God, and I respect that. But this idea of an all-powerful, watching being that's controlling our moves and giving us a chance to say he's the greatest so we get into some eternal heaven—that just doesn't work for me, man. I got a real problem with it. I see the value of religion and what it offers to people as a cushion and I don't want to step on that. On the other hand, I've seen where I grew up how it becomes separatist, and I get quite aggravated and antagonistic. I see religion more as a truck stop on your way to figuring out who you are.[1]

The "cushion" Pitt speaks about, which he also refers to as a "pillow" against our fear of death, is a concept that resonates with atheists and skeptics alike. But I strongly disagree with their entire premise. Why would inventing *something* after death be preferable to nothing? If nothing is all that awaits us when we die, who would care? We'd be gone. I've been knocked out for surgery. It's delightful nothingness. The idea that there might actually be something after this life is far more terrifying for the unbeliever. Hence, most atheists and naturalists have insisted upon nothingness to sooth their own frightened minds, and who can blame them? But how much better that God takes the initiative to point out the afterlife in Scripture. We can run but we cannot hide because while we may do our best to deny it, God has set eternity in the hearts of men (Eccl. 3:11).

Over ten years ago, singer and songwriter Jackson Browne gave an interview amidst teachers and middle-school students. Because his lyrics taught me to go a little deeper than I might have as an eighth grader, and because I played his first three albums until they were completely worn out, his interview caught my attention. In it he stated, "One of the things that Christianity believes that I can't really adhere to is the idea that unless you are a Christian, you won't go to heaven. That's leaving an awful lot of people out."[2]

Scripture doesn't say much about how God will deal with people who haven't had a chance to hear or fully understand the truth of Christ, thus who haven't had the opportunity to straight-up reject Him. I often wonder what makes us think that everyone who responds to God— from every nation, tribe, people, and language—should look and sound the same. And if they don't agree with us on all points, why do we think they're hopeless or that their blood is on our hands? As far as I can tell, we've never been invited to assume the role of the Holy Spirit.

The first two chapters of the book of Romans are the closest thing we have to an explanation of how God will deal fairly with those who haven't had an opportunity to become "fully accountable" to Him.

Paul first points out that everyone, whether they've heard the name of Jesus or not, is accountable to God to some degree, purely through the revelation of nature (1:20). Not only that, but evidence for God moves beyond nature and creation. Paul points out that there is a measure of accountability through a "God-consciousness" we are all born with (2:15).

Obviously, not everyone has been given a good understanding of God's Word, nor will they be held accountable in the same way as those who have. But that doesn't make truths of Scripture any less true. Some students are graced with exceptional math programs, while others are not, but this does not make the rules of calculus any less true.

To come down hard on issues that are not fully clear lacks intellectual integrity. It misrepresents God's nature and unnecessarily fuels doubt, confusion, and the atheist position. Whenever I wonder if God can be fair about such things without my help, I remember what one of my cousins, who has been in foreign missions for over three decades, told me years ago. When I asked about this troubling concept of who has heard and who hasn't, Steve's simple response was, "I'm pretty sure God will be able to sort it all out." What a concept.

There's mixed opinion in the church about hell too, with some taking an eternal-punishment viewpoint, and others that of annihilation. Both agree on the concept of hell, it's on the duration they disagree. I've heard clever and convincing arguments made from Scripture on both sides. I've also heard differing opinions about the debate itself. Some feel that if we whitewash the reality of hell, people will not take seriously the idea of separation from God. On the other hand, the notion of relentless, eternal torture is a major contributor to the atheistic stand against Christianity in general. No one is suggesting that we change what God's Word says in order to accommodate naysayers on either side, only that we be very sure about what we're willing to go to the wall for and why.

I probably don't think about heaven as much as I should. Most of us don't in our busy lives of the concrete here and now. We don't really want to. As Woody Allan so aptly put it, he is not afraid of dying; he just doesn't want to be around when it happens. But I see how contemplating death changes when we're facing adversity, mourning the loss of a loved one, or staring death in the face. That's what makes Christopher Hitchens's remarks to Anderson Cooper so mysteriously brazen. Like it or not, every one of us is but a breath away from death at any given moment.

Pascal's statement, "If you gain, you gain all; if you lose, you lose nothing,"[3] is a reminder of the high stakes involved with a belief in God. It is an intellectual approach to faith in God that is based solely on probability, reason, and logic—three commodities that tend to run in short supply when we are struggling with doubt. The intellect is an important aspect of our faith, but like all things, it must be kept in balance, because worshiping at the altar of intellectualism invites a different kind of problem.

The Atheist Debate

I love to see great intellects at work. Few things fascinate me more than watching people who are regarded as experts in their field debate a topic, especially when I disagree with them. I like to see where people are coming from, how they got there, and what I'm not missing. I appreciated Richard Dawkins's preface to the first edition of *The Selfish Gene*. He said he chose to speak in layman's terms, resisting the urge to use "technical jargon" that only trained biologists could comprehend. He wondered why all journals don't do the same. Then he added that while he assumed the layman who reads his book has no specialized knowledge, he did not assume him to be stupid. *Thank you, Professor Dawkins.*

The problem with great intellects, though, is the enormous egos they're often saddled with. It can become so oppressive that it clouds their ability to remain open-minded, the very thing they accuse Christians of not being. And the stakes are high. In fact, after watching the Anderson Cooper interview and reading the book by Hitchens's younger brother, former atheist Peter Hitchens, *Rage Against God*—a rebuttal to Christopher's views—I felt compelled to pray for Christopher Hitchens. And I wasn't alone. By publicly coming out so strongly against the possibility of God, Hitchens had essentially painted himself into a corner. Pride alone may have prevented him from changing his position, at least publicly.

Time magazine hosted a debate between Richard Dawkins and geneticist Francis Collins, former atheist and director of the Human Genome Project. After Dawkins admitted the universe is at present unexplainable, *Time* asked him, "Could the answer be God?"

Dawkins said, "There could be something incredibly grand and incomprehensible and beyond our present understanding."

Collins replied, "That's God."[4]

In a 2012 interview, atheist poet Jennifer Michael Hecht stated:

> I don't believe anything supernatural—no God, no ghosts, no unified spirit of life coursing through all things. But I do believe in love, free will, inexplicable feelings of connectedness, and human irrationalism, and I value the experience of sentient living with a genuine reverence. I am awed by the universe, with its infinitesimal particles and billions of galaxies. Also, I am awed by the unfathomable depth of the human imagination and force of feeling.[5]

As I watched her speak to the Harvard Humanists, an atheist club I don't expect to be invited to speak at any time soon, I was struck by her belief that humanists tend to focus "too much" on science. She believes, and the historian/anthropologist in her bears this out, that if they want to understand people better, they should focus more on art and culture.

As a Christian, I understand the intelligence of her statements that essentially call our attention to the fact that both creation and conscience evidence a Creator. And while the logical argument can be made for this outside of Scripture, the first two chapters of Romans teach us as much.

Unlike many atheists of the past (who at least took pity on poor, unenlightened Christians), these new crusaders insist that if one is not part of the solution—which is stomping out all facets of religion—one is part of the problem. To these New Atheists, faith is self-delusion and the catalyst to social injustice, abuse, and war.

Indeed, there have been plenty of false prophets to litter the landscape. Jesus referred to them as wolves in sheep's clothing—*Vipers. Snakes.* They inflict pain by distorting the truth, as all religious hypocrites do. As a child, I would often hear my pastor, Jay Kesler, say to the skeptic, "Tell me about your God. I don't think I believe in him either."

Several years ago, I was cleaning up breakfast dishes and getting my kids off to school when I noticed the morning news ending and the *Regis and Kathie Lee* show beginning. I was about to switch off the set when the announcer said that Carl Sagan would be making a visit to the show, so I decided to watch. Knowing that Kathie Lee was a professing Christian and Dr. Sagan a nonbeliever, I decided to stay tuned and see how the dynamics of the interview played out. As Sagan spoke in his trademark gentle manner about the cosmos, evolution, and his latest book, Kathie Lee listened politely. When he finally finished speaking, she said something like, "Excuse me, Dr. Sagan. Can you tell me what got the big bang started?"

Sagan broke into a dissertation about the billions of years it took for the universe to expand, and again Kathie Lee listened, then politely asked, "But what got all *that* started?" Again, Sagan explained about the immense heat that forced dense matter outward and Kathie Lee listened, and yet again asked, "But what got all *that* started?" The two of them went on like this for several moments and I noticed the doctor's patience wearing thin. Finally, to put an end to her incessant questioning, he simply stated, "We just don't know." This was what Kathie Lee was looking for. As she thanked him, I felt almost embarrassed for Sagan, the brilliant scientist reduced to a fool on national TV by the perky Kathie Lee. As the psalmist so eloquently stated, "The fool says in his heart, 'There is no God'" (14:1).

To his credit, Sagan wasn't nearly as hostile as his contemporaries have been known to be. I saw an interview in which he admitted that an atheist would have to know more than he knew because an atheist is someone who *knows* there is no God. Indeed, I agree. An atheist would have to transcend time and space to have this kind of information. Only then could he assert that there isn't, nor has there ever been, a God. Only a fool would tip his hand and expose this kind of ego. Agnosticism is far more palatable.

There are plenty of scientists, such as John Lennox and John Polkinghorne, and many other brilliant minds worth listening to who find their way onto Socrates in the City, a monthly event created by Eric Metaxas where successful professionals gather in New York City to discuss the weighty issues of life. Many of them believe in theistic evolution or that God used evolution when He created the world. Indeed, I'd be open to this too. I don't want to be deluded or misinformed, and on some levels I already believe in evolution. Adaptation, which refers to changes made in order to better suit a particular environment, is the simplest example of that, though plenty of scientists assert that with enough time, microevolution can become macroevolution. I am, however, still waiting for the proverbial missing link, the proof positive of genetic mutation, because in the end, what takes more faith . . . believing God started the universe or believing that it all came from nothing? There is not one piece of empirical evidence proving that something can originate from nothing. And if society's moral compass is merely the result of Darwinism, and altruism exists simply because it perpetuates a species, then there are absolutely no absolutes—which, of course, is a contradiction of terms and precisely the problem I have with the atheist option. All it has to offer is a lot of nothing.

Looking Deeper

1. What is the best argument for the existence of God?
2. What is the best argument against the existence of God?
3. Where do these arguments originate, and how should they be handled?

Chapter 8

IS JESUS GOD?

Returning from a conference several years ago, I boarded a plane for Chicago's O'Hare airport. As I settled into my window seat for the three-hour flight home, I was reminded of how delightful it is when you discover that the seat between you and the aisle guy is empty. But, just as the flight attendants were finishing the overhead-compartment slam, one last traveler burst onto the plane and took his spot in the only seat left. *Nuts.*

I tried to concentrate on my reading, but my peripheral vision told me that the bundle of energy sitting next to me had already sized up the other passengers and was now resting his gaze on me.

"So," he said loudly, breaking the ice. "What do you do?"

This should be an easy question, but I often find it challenging. It's not that I'm ashamed of the gospel, but I am ashamed of people who've attached themselves to it and misrepresented it, keeping others away in the process. And I am by no means alone as I seek to do serious damage control. So I treaded lightly. "I speak at women's conferences."

He looked down, noticed the apologetics book that sat open on my lap, and said, "Oh. You're a Christian, right?"

"Yes," I answered.

"Cool," he said, nodding his head as if he thought I could use some approval. "That's cool." Then he paused, turned to me again, and said, "I'm Jewish."

"Cool," I said, returning the nod. "That's cool."

With that settled we smiled at each other and sat in silence for a few moments, waiting to see who would venture out next. He did . . . and big time. He said, "You know . . . I realize Christians say that Jesus is God, and his apostles said he was God, but I've always wondered if Jesus himself actually claimed to be God." He could not have brought up a more intelligent point, and these are the moments when as Christians we can be glad our faith is built on more than conjecture, self-deception, and wishful thinking. No matter how desperately revisionists want to rewrite the past, Christianity is born out of history, facts, and reason. If Christianity were not rooted in history, it would have degenerated like any other mythology, with Jesus going the way of Zeus, Odin, and Thor. And while there are plenty of people who wish that would happen, the staggering rate at which the church is growing within even the communistic confines of places like China, proves otherwise.

I told him that large portions of the New Testament, the earliest copies dating back to the contemporaries of Christ, were written by close friends of Jesus. They heard His conversations and recorded many of them.

In John 10, Jesus said, "I and the Father are one" (v. 30). In John 14, He said, "Anyone who has seen me has seen the Father" (v. 9). Even the enemies of Jesus understood His claims of deity when they picked up stones and said, "We're stoning you because you, mere man, claim to be God." I pointed out that even the prophets of His own Jewish faith announced Jesus' arrival hundreds of years before He came, though many Jews are still waiting for these graphic Scriptures to be fulfilled or believe they refer to the Jewish people themselves. In Isaiah 7:14, Isaiah said He would be called Immanuel, which means "God with us"; Isaiah 53 is a virtual blueprint for the coming Messiah.

In Revelation 21:6, Jesus refers to Himself as the Alpha and the Omega; in John 8:58, He says, "Before Abraham was born, I am"; in

John 14:6, He says He is the Way, the Truth, and the Life. Jesus knew who He was and was not afraid to say it.

As we talked, I thought of how glad I was that I'd asked enough of my own questions to intelligently try to answer his. Part of my search involved pain, but nothing compared to a Jewish man or his family, who might mistakenly, though understandably, equate Hitler's Final Solution with Christianity. God will have to sort all of that out one day, but much like my seatmate, I too had wanted to know if there was a God, if Jesus was God, if the Bible was God's Word, and what sets Christianity apart from other world religions and philosophies. I had already come to a place in my own life where I was able to say with the apostle Peter, "For me, it's Christ or nothing." One day, Jesus had asked Peter if he planned to abandon Him like some of the other disciples, but Peter knew there was no place else to go. He had exhausted his options, which is a fabulous place to be, and asked where else he could possibly go. "Simon Peter answered him, 'Lord, to whom shall we go? You have the words of eternal life. We have come to believe and to know that you are the Holy One of God'" (John 6:68–69).

It's not that other religions and philosophies don't have something of value to contribute to the human dialogue. There's nothing wrong with atheists arguing for logic and reason. In fact, there is everything right about it. Clearly, many of these worldviews can offer wise guidelines to shape a healthy lifestyle. But the question is, what makes Jesus unique? Whether or not we view Him to be the fulfillment of the prophets and the Messiah who existed before the foundations of the earth doesn't change the truth about who He really is. He certainly raised the bar, though, as a prophet and teacher, never compromising His conviction of right and wrong, instead tempering it with the perfect balance of forgiveness and compassion.

One of my favorite biblical narratives is about the woman caught in adultery. About to be stoned for her infraction, Jesus doesn't defend her actions. He defends *her*. And in the process, He silenced those who were in no position to judge. Though some of the earliest and most reliable manuscripts do not include this narrative, its message fits beautifully into the flow of the truths of Scripture and illustrates God's view of both sin and the sinner.

But Jesus claimed to be more than a wise teacher, which is what sets Him apart from other religious leaders throughout history. As Josh McDowell points out, "Buddha did not claim to be God; Moses never said that he was Yahweh; Mohammed did not identify himself as Allah; and nowhere will you find Zoroaster claiming to be Ahura Mazda. Yet Jesus, the carpenter from Nazareth, said that he who has seen Him (Jesus) has seen the Father (John 14:9)."[1]

The great intellect and literary scholar C. S. Lewis, who referred to himself as the most reluctant convert in all of England, pointed out that when it comes to Christ, our options are few. Some would like to put Jesus in a box, conceding only that He was a good man or a good teacher. However, His claim to deity will not allow that. He either was who He claimed to be—God—or He was not . . . in which case He must have been a lunatic or a liar, but by no means a good teacher.

Lewis wrote, "You can shut Him up for a fool, you can spit at Him and kill Him as a demon; or you can fall at His feet and call Him Lord and God. But let us not come with any patronising nonsense about His being a great human teacher. He has not left that open to us. He did not intend to."[2]

When our plane finally landed and we were cattle-prodded off, my new friend turned to me one last time. Maybe it was the tiny bottle of airline spirits talking, but he smiled and said, "Pray for me." Then he disappeared into the Chicago throng. I wasn't sure if his request was genuine or if he was just humoring me, but I was serious when I told him I would. When I arrived home, I realized God was serious too. During our chat, the man had told me he was an actor and had just finished filming a cold-medicine commercial, and though I will not pretend to know much about marketing strategies for cold medicines,

God's marketing strategy became extraordinarily clear. In the days that followed, I must have seen his commercial on TV at least twice, if not three times a day. And each time I saw it, I stopped everything I was doing and prayed that Christ would open his eyes and show him not only the immense love He has for all of us, but also who He really is . . . the Messiah, his Messiah and mine—"For in Christ all the fullness of the Deity lives in bodily form" (Col. 2:9).

In his book, *The Big Story*, Justin Buzzard, a hip pastor from Silicon Valley, states that anyone who really thinks it through cannot remain neutral about Jesus. Either Christ is who He claimed to be or He is not. Buzzard points out that all religious leaders come with *good advice*, which isn't a bad thing. But Jesus is the only one who comes with *good news* about forgiveness. Good advice is never a bad thing, but which would you rather have, Buzzard asks, good advice or good news?

Looking Deeper

1. What makes Jesus unique?
2. What makes faith in Christ challenging?
3. Why does faith in Christ matter?

Chapter 9

IS THE BIBLE GOD'S WORD?

One of the best ways to learn a topic is to teach it. Years ago, I was slated to give a lecture on the reliability of the Scriptures for a leadership training conference, and it became one of the most powerful faith-strengthening exercises of my life. God's Word may claim to be God's Word, but circular logic only goes so far.

In his book, *A Ready Defense*, Josh McDowell does a great job of explaining how scholars test the authenticity of ancient documents. By examining the oldest copies and matching them up against the copies still in circulation today, they are able to conduct textual evaluations. For example, Caesar's *The Gallic Wars* was written around 100–44 BC. The earliest copy we possess is AD 900. That leaves a time span of about 950 years. The New Testament, however, was written about AD 40–100. The earliest copy we possess is AD 125. The time span is about twenty-five years, well within the lifetime of the contemporaries of Jesus, thus easily verifiable.

With the discovery of the Dead Sea Scrolls in 1947, the reliability and authenticity of the Old Testament were further affirmed for scholars. A comparison of the book of Isaiah as copied by a group of Jewish scribes living in a communal setting in Qumran around 150 BC–AD 70 with the book of Isaiah in our Bibles today shows staggering consistency.

There is no other document that has endured the kind of scrutiny throughout history that the New Testament has. In fact, New Testament scholar F. F. Bruce states in *The New Testament Documents: Are They Reliable?* that the "evidence for our New Testament writings is ever so much greater than the evidence for many writings of classical authors, the authenticity of which no one dreams of questioning. And if the New Testament were a collection of secular writings, their authenticity would generally be regarded as beyond all doubt."[1]

Even secular scholars must concede on much of the evidence. But in general, most objections don't come from people who take the time to study the empirical data. Many would rather launch objections that are typically less about firm evidence and more about hunches, personal bias, and bad information. This is why, when it comes to evaluating objections to the New Testament, we must make sure that the objections leveled are coming from New Testament scholars and those who've actually studied the Scriptures.

Moral Stories

To move from a God who knows us to a God who wants us to know Him may not be much of a stretch, but determining *what* He wants us to know about Him and how we come to know it can become a real source of confusion. And for some, that confusion has threatened their faith. Skeptics ask, wouldn't an all-powerful God make things clear? But a better question might be, what keeps God's truth from being clear? Philosopher J. L. Schellenberg uses the term, "divine hiddenness" for the argument of unbelief which states that if God were really there we'd all believe in Him.

Jesus validates this argument but takes it a step further by making the point that it isn't simply a matter of the intellect when it comes to unbelief. Addressing this issue in the New Testament, Jesus says, "This is why I speak to them in parables: 'Though seeing, they do not see; though hearing, they do not hear or understand.'" Then, quoting the Old Testament prophet Isaiah, he continues, "You will be ever hearing but never understanding; you will be ever seeing but never perceiving. For this people's heart has become calloused; they hardly hear with their ears, and they have closed their eyes" (Matt. 13:13–15). The apostle Paul goes on to ask, "Has not God made foolish the wisdom of the world?" (1 Cor. 1:20). These passages strongly indicate that faith isn't simply about the intellect, though the intellect is certainly important.

In general, we can clear much of the confusion away when it comes to understanding the Scriptures by sticking to basic hermeneutic principles for interpreting a text. Simply asking who wrote the text in question, to whom it was written, what it meant to them, and what it means to us today can erase half the confusion when it comes to biblical interpretation. A striking example of biblical extremism recently flooded the news when poor hermeneutics turned deadly for a snake-handling preacher. But our mistaken interpretations don't need to be that blatant to be dangerous to our faith.

While the Scriptures declare themselves to be *God-breathed*, what people often want to know is if the Bible should be taken literally. In general, the old adage, "If the literal sense makes good sense, seek no other sense, lest you come up with nonsense," is probably a good rule of thumb. However, that's not to say the Bible doesn't contain figures of speech or personal perspectives by those giving their accounts. The Bible contains history as well as poetry, allegory, and so on. The Bible also contains hyperbole, using exaggeration to make a point, and includes anthropomorphism, ascribing human attributes to God, among other figures of speech. When my daughter was young and I told her she needed new shoes because hers were getting small, she didn't have a psychological meltdown wondering how shoes can shrink. Rarely do we suggest we watched a gorgeous earth-rotate, even though we're well aware that the sun doesn't actually set. Not recognizing when figures of speech are used would be a mistake.

The Scriptures were written by men who were inspired by the Holy

Spirit who kept the integrity of His truth in place without erasing their human touch. Certainly, God could have written His Word without us, but including people in the creative process validates His desire to have people involved.

Second Chronicles uses classic anthropomorphic language: "For the eyes of the LORD range throughout the earth to strengthen those whose hearts are fully committed to him" (16:9). Though this remains one of my favorite Scriptures with regard to God's omniscience, omnipotence, and omnipresence, I have yet to hear credible reports of giant eyes in the western sky.

It may surprise the music director at church that singing God's praises forever includes rightly acknowledging Him and not just singing hymns. And telling the congregation that in heaven we'll all be singing—just like this—forever and ever, doesn't always sweeten the deal for a person like me. For the musically challenged, the one who thinks we'd be just fine with two stanzas instead of six, this broader interpretation is welcome news. It's the same with passages such as 1 Thessalonians 4:17. "We who are still alive and are left will be caught up together with them in the clouds to meet the Lord in the air" never sounded too appealing to me. I'm afraid of heights.

Demanding black and white in what are clearly gray areas causes not only confusion but division. In fact, skeptics often charge that the sheer number of church denominations proves that Christians can't agree among themselves what God's Word says. However, instead of looking at diversity among denominations as a reflection of confusion or problems, perhaps we should see the differences as a reflection of the creativity of God.

In the "Question and Answer" section of the April 2013 edition of *Today in the Word*, professor of theology David Rim puts a refreshing slant on our differences when he answers a reader's question about denominational differences this way:

Naturally, there is disagreement over how to understand the disagreements. But what if the diversity of our faith is not a sign of a lack of clarity in God's Word nor the inability of God's Spirit to guide us into all truth, but a reflection of the richness of our faith? What if the diversity of faith is a divinely designed means of opening as many kinds of doors for people of all cultures, languages, and socioeconomic status to enter into a relationship with Jesus Christ? What if the diversity of faith is a divinely appointed opportunity for us to accept the differences among us in love as a praise offering to a God who saves both the Jews and the Gentiles (Rom. 15:5–6)?[2]

Understanding It All

We aren't intended to understand it all. Our Creator hasn't chosen to give us all of the answers. We don't know what an infinite God does outside of the constraints of the time and space He created for us. We can't fathom what it means that Christ walked the earth fully God and fully man. We can't wrap our minds around the Trinity, a term never used in the earliest Scripture texts, though its essence is taught from beginning to end. I'm not even sure we do God justice referring to His nature as three *persons*, though I realize we have to call it something.

Insisting church be done this way or that purely because "that's the way we've always done it" isn't particularly helpful. Nor is holding on to a doctrine that is divisive, though not, as theologians put it, *salvific*, that is, able to impact someone's salvation.

There are essentials to our faith, and they are nonnegotiable, but they are also comparatively few. First Timothy 2 sums up the entire New Testament's position on Christ: "For there is one God and one mediator between God and mankind, the man Christ Jesus, who gave himself as a ransom for all people" (vv. 5–6).

There are plenty of negotiables too, though I've noticed that some scholars are more willing to negotiate than others. For example, in the Genesis account, the word *yom*, which is Hebrew for the word *day*, can refer to an age of time or a literal twenty-four-hour period. Both uses of the word are legitimate. I could say that it took me a day to paint my fence, or I could say that back in my parents' day they didn't have cell phones. Both uses of the word *day* are valid but mean very different things.

In the Old Testament, the use of the word *day* is also interchangeable and leaves many Christians disagreeing about the age of the earth. Is the world millions or billions of years old or does it simply appear that way? Churches have split on such issues, which is unfortunate because whether one takes an old or new earth view doesn't change one's status before God. Why not celebrate our diversity instead?

Speculating or questioning is never wrong, but demanding answers when God gives none exposes our obsession with control and gets us in trouble. The apostle Paul reminds us to keep our perspective on what is really important: "In Christ Jesus . . . the only thing that counts is faith expressing itself through love" (Gal. 5:6).

Questions regarding our faith are nothing to be ashamed of. On the contrary, they indicate a mind that's grappling with issues of substance. Faith that doesn't take reason and logic seriously can be in jeopardy of collapsing under pressure. After graduation, I ran into a friend from high school who was happy to tell me about his new faith in Christ. I congratulated him and asked if he was plugged in to solid Bible teaching. He said no. That was too confining. Instead, he was involved with a small group of people who got together regularly but not to study the Bible—they wanted to give the Spirit freedom to simply move amongst them without direction. Though disappointed, I wasn't too surprised when I later heard he had abandoned his new beliefs. He had obviously underestimated the power of the intellect with regard to our faith, thus he wasn't digging into knowledge. He lacked the depth that comes with asking questions about God and discovering the answers.

Intellectual doubt can usher in tremendous growth and insight. It can become a great opportunity to ask logical questions, beginning with, will I be open to what I discover? Remaining open-minded and teachable is a crucial aspect to all learning. The next question should be, what will I do with all that I've learned? Clearly, intellectual insight about our faith was never meant to make us smug or judgmental—two of the most annoying character traits a believer can possess, right up there with hypocrisy. Those who've been marinating in God's grace for a while may need to spend less time seeing Christianity as a privilege and more time seeing it as a responsibility. The apostle Paul warned us about that: "Knowledge puffs up while love builds up" (1 Cor. 8:1).

There are myriad books, classes, and lectures put together by some of the finest Christian apologists of our day. (See the suggested resources at the back of this book.) Remember, all questions are simply answers you've yet to discover, and in this sense, intellectual doubt becomes a gift—the perfect opportunity for our faith and convictions to be examined and strengthened.

Looking Deeper

1. What evidence for God, Jesus, and the Bible has impacted your faith the most?
2. How are faith and reason related?
3. How is faith increased and/or decreased?

Chapter 10

EMOTIONAL DOUBT

Of the three kinds of doubt—spiritual, intellectual and emotional— the most common by far, and the most troubling, is emotional doubt. It's also the most difficult to identify because damaged emotions often make it impossible to draw the distinction between what merely *feels* true and what actually *is* true.

Emotional doubt is equal in importance to spiritual and intellectual doubt, but I deal with it last because when we're struggling, it's crucial to rule out the other two sources of doubt first. And, again, I'll issue a warning here: when our emotions get involved, which they often do, getting a handle on the source of our doubt becomes much trickier than it sounds, purely because of doubt's subjective nature. It's often based on feelings and opinions rather than the facts.

Also, whenever possible, it's a good idea *not* to ask the big questions when we're struggling, because emotions can greatly skew our ability to reason. As I mentioned earlier, ask the big questions—Is there a God? What about evil?—when you're strong and feeling good. When you've had enough sleep, your kids are safely tucked in bed, and the boss just gave you raise, *then* ask where God is.

Clarifying the type of doubt we're struggling with can often be settled by asking ourselves a few simple but pointed questions. For example, is there a person I'm involved with in some way that if I were honest with myself I would find the relationship objectionable? Is there an activity that I engage in privately that I would never admit to in public? If the answer is yes to either of these questions, this could be sign of trouble in the spiritual realm. As I mentioned before, wrong or "sinful" behavior can become a powerful source of spiritual doubt. If, on the other hand, I'm dotting my i's and crossing my t's, spiritually speaking, yet I still sense spiritual fatigue or frustration, then there could be another source to my spiritual doubt, aka, spiritual warfare.

Both scenarios mentioned above, sin and spiritual warfare, can be greatly alleviated through quiet introspection and prayerful confession. Speaking to a trusted friend, a pastor, or a counselor who can offer guidance and support can bring tremendous relief as well.

If the problem is more tangible and cerebral, we might be experiencing intellectual doubt. We can confirm this by asking ourselves a different set of questions. For example, is what I am objecting to something I simply need to be more educated about? Is it a doctrinal issue? Do I find myself at odds with what I'm being taught? Does that tension keep me from engaging with other Christians?

Sometimes teachers or preachers can come down so hard on an issue that we're surprised to learn that equally committed Christians disagree with them. Taking an apologetics course, reading a few books, or clicking on some useful websites (see suggested resources) can be incredibly effective at combating intellectual doubt by teaching us how to think for ourselves.

The Bible clearly differentiates between the emotions and the intellect when it comes to faith . . . which, for the doubter, is really good news. In fact, one of the most annoying statements a person struggling with doubt can hear another Christian make is *I'm so in love with Jesus.* The doubter, who is already frustrated, is now left wondering why they can't feel the love. I remind women that it's in these moments we should find solace in the fact that how we feel about God has very little to do with our actual status before Him. When Jesus said in John 14:23,

"Anyone who loves me will obey my teaching," He said absolutely nothing about how we might *feel* about it. Loving God may include the
emotions, and it will for some people more than others, but love in this
sense, according to Jesus, is an act of the will. It is a decision we make.
It is obedience.

But when the painful sting of doubt grips us and we've ruled out the
first two sources, it may be time to take a look at our emotions. This
may be a hard task, particularly for those who've become adept at sti-
fling their feelings and burying their pain.

Even now, after all I've learned, I continue to be amazed at how my
emotions can influence my reason. If I'm nervous, let's say, about my
daughter driving alone at night or the results of a medical report or even
something as "seemingly" insignificant as a Green Bay Packers play-off
game, everything I process is impacted: my mood, my thoughts, my
motivation. While I wait for resolution to my issue, I find myself vulnerable and concerned about things I didn't think about the day before.
If I'm under enough pressure, I might even feel as though I'm getting a
touch of the flu.

However, when things finally get resolved and the strain is relieved,
my recovery is always quite miraculous. The things that had weighed
so heavily on me only hours before are often completely forgotten, and
that's when I'm again reminded of how unreliable thoughts and feelings
can be under pressure. Stress, illness, fatigue, grief, anger, fear, loneli-
ness, and even hormones can alter our emotions and impact how we
think. And this is precisely how and why emotional doubt creeps in.

It's not uncommon for people under pressure to suddenly come face-
to-face with issues they've long buried. In their fragile state, a mere
scent or sound can conjure up painful associations and push them over
the edge. Caught completely off guard, women come to me and ask
what's wrong with their faith. In these types of situations, I assure them
that it's merely their "woundedness" speaking. Validating their pain,
whether from some sort of disappointment, abuse, or abandonment,

is not only essential not only to their emotional healing but to their faith-building process as well.

Emotions can be highly unreliable, but that doesn't make them any less significant. Years ago, I committed to memory a statement by C. S. Lewis that speaks to doubt. In *Mere Christianity*, he said, "Faith . . . is the art of holding on to things your reason has once accepted, in spite of your changing moods."[1] Lewis knew how unreliable emotions could be, yet as sensible as his statement was, even he was caught off guard by the depths of his own grief as he faced the death of his wife due to cancer. He torturously puzzled over his sudden inability to reason in light of his pain and stated in his journal, *A Grief Observed*, "Feelings, and feelings, and feelings. Let me try thinking instead."[2]

Reason is often the first thing to go when we're struggling with raw emotion. Pain has cut many strong men to the quick. We hold John the Baptist up as a symbol of strength and clarity of faith, but while he was in prison, fueled by exhaustion and disillusionment, he too struggled with doubt. From his miserable cell, he sent his messengers to Jesus and asked, "Are you the one who is to come, or should we expect someone else?" (Matt. 11:3). John had boldly proclaimed the coming of Christ just days earlier. Now in chains, he barely recognized Him. Pain will do that.

Two months into my second pregnancy, I began to bleed. I frantically dialed my doctor to tell him what was happening. I was sure he'd make it better by telling me to go to the hospital or meet him at his office. Instead, after asking me a few questions and listening to my answers, he instructed me to lie down, take it easy, and wait and see what happens.

"Wait and see?" I tried to calm myself as I hung up the phone, but I was overcome by fear and utter powerlessness. There had to be something he could do. He was a specialist, a man of science who dealt with high-risk pregnancies every day. He had state-of-the-art medical equipment at his disposal and a well-trained staff. Yet, all he could offer was "wait and see"? The depth of my despair was overwhelming as I felt the life drain from my body and realized there was nothing anyone could do. It was over.

My despair quickly turned to anger, as I asked what kind of God would create a world where such pain is possible. All reason was pushed aside, and I had no interest in contemplating what life would actually be like if we were simply robots incapable of discerning between pleasure and pain. In fact, robotics suddenly sounded very appealing. I argued with God and pointed out to Him that at least John the Baptist's pain ended quickly before his head was served on a platter.

Practicing the discipline of gratitude would have perhaps broadened my perspective, but in that moment, I didn't feel particularly grateful to God. Rather, my bitter thoughts wondered why I should feel grateful for anything. I never asked to be born in the first place.

Even Old Testament heroes Moses and Elijah became emotionally wrought and wanted to die. In Numbers 11, Moses was one unhappy man in charge of many unhappy people. After he'd become a hero for leading them out of captivity, the Israelites complained incessantly. For one thing, the manna that God had provided for them to eat in the wilderness, which had at one point been a miraculous provision, was now becoming just another problem. They were sick of it, and began complaining as they glorified the past: "We remember the fish we ate in Egypt at no cost—also the cucumbers, melons, leeks, onions and garlic. But now we have lost our appetite; we never see anything but this manna!" (Num. 11:5–6). *If only we were back in Egypt. Remember how good we had it? Never mind we were in bondage to the Egyptian whip.*

Moses was overworked and underappreciated, and at the end of his rope when he complained to God. His candor is refreshing.

Why have you brought this trouble on your servant? What have I done to displease you that you put the burden of all these people on me? Did I conceive all these people? Did I give them birth? . . . If this is how you are going to treat me, please go ahead and kill me—if I have found favor in your eyes—and do not let me face my own ruin. (Num. 11:11, 15)

The story of Elijah's emotional roller coaster, recorded in 1 Kings 19, is easy to relate to as well. The prophet, who had just commanded fire to come down from heaven as he boldly opposed the worship of Baal, was now running for his life. The crazy Queen Jezebel wanted him dead. So he sat down under a tree and, like Moses, asked God to take his life: "He came to a broom bush, sat down under it and prayed that he might die. 'I have had enough, Lord. . . . Take my life; I am no better than my ancestors'" (v. 4). *Just kill me now, Lord!*

What's immensely comforting in these passages is God's tender response. He didn't punish Elijah or Moses for their emotional meltdowns and doubts. They wanted to give up! They wanted to die, and they blamed God for everything. Yet, what God heard was their authentic cry of brokenness, and what He offered were practical solutions to heal their fragile state. To Elijah, God provided food and rest (1 Kings 19:6–7). To Moses, God introduced a brand new word—*delegate*—a word every frazzled control-freak leader should have in his or her vocabulary. God instructed Moses to bring the elders down to the Tent of Meeting where He would anoint them to serve—"They will share the burden of the people with you so that you will not have to carry it alone" (Num. 11:17).

To John, Jesus sent his disciples to bring him a powerful word of assurance: "Jesus replied, 'Go back and report to John what you hear and see: The blind receive sight, the lame walk, those who have leprosy are cleansed, the deaf hear, the dead are raised, and the good news is proclaimed to the poor. Blessed is anyone who does not stumble on account of me'" (Matt. 11:4–6). Jesus says, "Hang in there. Be encouraged!"

In my anger and sadness on the day I lost my pregnancy, I tried my best to become an atheist, but it wouldn't take. In my agony, nothing in me longed for God. *Not* believing felt like a much easier path to take. Damaged emotions often gravitate toward hunches rather than sound knowledge. *It doesn't feel likely that a good God would allow this pain; therefore, He must not exist.*

Maybe, while contemplating God's existence and his own, what Descartes meant to say was, *I hurt, therefore I am.* My pain made me keenly aware of my own existence, and whether I liked it or not, I knew in that moment God was there too. In fact, in order to stop believing in God, I knew I'd have some serious backpedaling to do. I'd have to disregard a lifetime of evidence to suddenly become a nonbeliever. But emotional doubt is less about facts and much more about feelings, which is why learning to distinguish between facts and feelings is essential to the healing and faith-building process.

Looking Deeper

1. Why is emotional doubt so difficult to identify?
2. How have your emotions been damaged or strengthened?
3. What part do emotions play in the realm of our faith?

Chapter 11

DOUBT AND DISILLUSIONMENT

Another powerful aspect to emotional doubt is disillusionment. The sneaking suspicion that God cannot be trusted can usually be traced back to the moment we first sense a disconnect between the good God we pray to and the bad things that happen—that God isn't really as good as we thought. Even a learned scholar and skeptic such as Bart Ehrman admits that abandoning his faith was primarily due to his inability to reconcile a good God with bad things that happen. Nothing calls God's character into question faster than our disappointment with Him, which is precisely when disillusionment rears its ugly head.

Maybe it's a cultural phenomenon or simply a sign of the times, but one of the dangers of living in our sophisticated twenty-first century is being lulled into a false sense of security. We all feel entitled to success, with secular people pinning their hopes on science or themselves, and believers pinning their hopes on God. But whether through test tube, old-fashioned hard work, prayer, or all three, we all want to control our own destinies.

Having been lulled into this false sense of security myself, I felt certain the doctor could save my second pregnancy. But he couldn't, and he didn't, and the pain of my adversity was mistaken for God's absence. Many Christians living in the West today maintain a theology that teeters on the edge of "prosperity" doctrine, a phenomenon that isn't nearly as prevalent in less developed cultures or in societies past. And it's a phenomenon we'd be hard-pressed to defend scripturally.

Professor John Koessler is one of the clearest-thinking Christians I've ever heard address the topic of disillusionment. In an interview, the author of *The Surprising Grace of Disappointment* pointed out the dangers of cheapening the promises of Christ and developing a narcissistic spirituality.

If we move away from the clear and basic truths of Scripture, we tend to veer off course into extremism. But if we fix our gaze on what God has promised, rather than on what He hasn't promised, we can learn how to pray with confidence and claim the strength and direction He offers us no matter what happens in our lives. The power of the Holy Spirit isn't a wild stallion that we need to tame in order to suit our needs. Nor can we ever fully predict God's will or how He'll answer our prayers. If we believe that we can, it sets us up for all sorts of doubt and disillusionment.

In a biography of our seventh president, Andrew Jackson, we're told that his father had been killed in a logging accident three weeks before Andrew's birth. When Andrew and his brother Robert were teenagers living in North Carolina, they were arrested by British officers for passing notes. They nearly starved to death as prisoners of war and also contracted smallpox. Their mother fought for her young sons' release, and although Andrew eventually recovered from smallpox, Robert died. An older brother had recently died in the war, and six months after securing the release of Andrew and Robert, their mother died of cholera. Andrew Jackson was orphaned by the age of fourteen.

One stroll through a cemetery should remind each one of us how little control we really have in life. My mom recently pointed out an old cemetery near her house with five small graves holding five children from the same family. Each child had died before reaching the age of ten.

As I looked at the graves, I thought about how families who emigrated like mine did from Scandinavia and settled as pioneers in places like Wisconsin, as mine did, faced these kinds of adversities regularly. They had large families and all but expected that some of their children would die. They lived with a gritty realism that we try to gloss over. They knew how little control they had over life and death, and although losing a family member couldn't have been any easier for them, they were always aware of the risks and fragility of life.

When our expectation of God's involvement in our lives moves into the realm of extremism, whether we expect too much or too little—and we're often guilty of both—we endanger the health of our faith. It cannot be overstated to say that many a faith has succumbed to emotional shipwreck the moment things did not turn out the way someone thought they should. But when we learn to bring every concern to God and ask for His best for us, in any circumstance, whether pleasant or painful, we will become liberated, and our faith will steer back on course with a renewed vigor and vision.

It's easy to become distracted and lose sight of God in our self-sufficient culture, and doubts become the natural consequence of that self-reliance, obscuring our vision even further. Emotionally speaking, in some ways, simply rejecting the sovereignty of God can become the path of least resistance. It can make things easier at times, or at least a little less complicated.

We might even become reluctant to thank God for the good things just so we won't have to blame Him for the bad. When bad things happen, we tend to tiptoe around the emotionally charged subject of God's control, lest we find Him culpable in some way. We want our God to be all about goodness, kindness, and fair play. We thank Him for safe travels, sunshine on our picnics, and parking spots next to the mall entrance. And, indeed, Scripture says it's good to give thanks to the Lord. In fact, I've never met a person who makes a practice of being grateful who hasn't been pleasant to be around. The book of James tells us that every good and perfect gift comes from God.

However, the natural consequence to all this thankfulness can become disillusionment when suffering surfaces. We don't know how to rationalize a good God's involvement, so we brush off the unfortunate details of these inconsistencies with platitudes, like, "Well, we just live in a fallen world" or "Sometimes God just allows things like this to happen."

These types of statements may be helpful for some, but personally, I've never found them able to satisfy my understanding of what a completely sovereign God is all about. They seem inconsistent, stopping logic halfway through its course, and for me, the emotional fallout was overwhelming.

When King David faced serious hardship in his life, he didn't deem it necessary to skirt the issue of God's involvement, as though somehow the Lord's sensibilities needed protecting. Instead, he reverenced God by acknowledging Him to be bigger than his circumstances. David knew that God was in the midst of his pain and working through him to accomplish a greater goal: "I know, LORD, that your laws are righteous, and that in faithfulness you have afflicted me. May your unfailing love be my comfort, according to your promise to your servant. Let your compassion come to me that I may live, for your law is my delight" (Ps. 119:75–77).

What other conclusion can be drawn from Moses when he says to God in Psalm 90:14–15, "Satisfy us in the morning with your unfailing love, that we may sing for joy and be glad all our days. Make us glad for as many days as you have afflicted us, for as many years as we have seen trouble"?

Job's wife wasn't guilty of denying God's presence in the midst of her husband's pain. What Job took issue with was her emotional response. He called her a fool when she suggested he simply curse God and die. Then he asked, "Shall we accept the good from God, and not the trouble?" (Job 2:10).

Accepting difficulties doesn't mean we need to be happy about them, nor does it mean we shouldn't do what we can to alleviate suffering. I'm all about making the best of every situation. But it does mean that in the scheme of things, God reserves the right to weave into our lives events that will be purposeful—both for our growth and the growth of others. When we're hurting, a mental assent to this truth may have to suffice because our emotions may not be up to the task. When we allow feelings to shape our theology, our faith becomes a very shallow well to draw from, and doubt and disillusionment are not far behind.

Inconvenience of Someone Else's Rules

Skewed as it may be, most of us are born with a sense of fair play. Faith is tested when life's scales tip out of balance, particularly when it inconveniences us. Like most people, I'm somewhat of a paradox with regard to what fairness looks like. On the one hand, I'm a stickler for following rules. Nothing makes me crazier when I'm playing a board game than teammates who say, "Oh, just give them the point. They were close enough." On more than one occasion, I've been known to argue like a prosecutor before a jury and point out the rules that are clearly printed on the box. (I might get invited to more parties if I didn't.) However, this stickler for rules tends to struggle with authority, just a tad, when the rules no longer *make sense.*

Years ago, I began to suspect I might have a problem with rules and authority when my kids and I decided to go for a swim at the public pool. Both kids were old enough to go off on their own, so I spread out my towel, adjusted my headphones, and lay back to soak up the rays.

A few moments later, a teenaged lifeguard tapped me lightly on the shoulder. "Excuse me, ma'am," he said politely. As I opened my eyes and squinted against the brilliant blue, I noticed he was inches from my face and holding a tiny piece of paper. "May I take your gum for you?" I had seen the massive sign listing the rules of the pool when I walked through the locker room earlier that day. "No chewing gum," it said. *Good idea*, I thought as I walked past the showers, chewing discreetly. *Kids can be so careless.*

Resisting the urge to stick my gum on the zinced-white nose of the boy who'd just called me *ma'am*, I placed it in the paper and forced myself to thank him. As I watched him saunter away, I wondered, *Did he honestly think I'd drop my gum on the ground or stick it under a deck chair when I was finished with it?* Whatever. Somewhat offended, I lay back on my towel and tried to let the music smooth over my offended pride. But then another thought hit me, this one involving the guy whose job it was to clean the multicolored globs from the pool drain. Surely he wasn't looking to split hairs over who should be allowed to chew gum and who shouldn't. (Darn those righteous thoughts.)

At some time or another, we all struggle with the inconvenience of someone else's authority. When it comes to the Almighty, the struggle can get even tougher. I can still smell the shoe rubber of my five-year-old daughter's brand-new pink jellies. She was so excited about her new sandals she could barely contain herself on the ride home from the store. Her excitement was short-lived, however, when after a few pirouettes through the living room she noticed the shoes beginning to pinch.

She sat down on the couch and looked at me. "Mom," she said, as she pointed to her heel, "they kind of hurt right here." I sat down beside her and suggested that maybe they were too small; maybe we should go back to the store and exchange them. The look on her face told me she didn't like the sound of that, and she made no attempt to conceal her displeasure. It was obvious she had no intention of parting with her brand-new hot-pink jellies. So, in my best Montessori voice, I tried to reason with her. I told her that we basically had two choices. She could wear her new jellies outside right away, in which case she would probably develop a blister and never want to wear them again, or she could be patient and allow me to exchange them for her, thus guaranteeing her long-term enjoyment. Then I waited. Looking back, I'm not sure what I expected from her—maybe something like, "Oh, Mother, you are ever so right." Instead, what I got was one of many reality checks my daughter was placed on this planet to deliver.

As she darted toward the door, she announced, "I'm going outside." I grabbed her hand and pulled her onto the couch. "Sit down," I said, this time more firmly. "Did you hear what I said? If you wear the shoes outside, we won't be able to return them, and if they give you blisters, you're never going to want to wear them again."

She looked down at her feet and back at me . . . then made a second attempt at a quick escape.

It's hard to know who was more disappointed as I pulled off the jellies, shoved them back into the box, and announced our plan to exchange them the next day. My daughter demanded to know why I was doing this, but nothing I said in that moment made sense to her. So, like all good parents whose bag of tricks is running low, I felt the words leave me before I could stop them: "Because I said so."

As I stood at the front window that day and watched my daughter sulk down the driveway in disgust, I thought of how, moments earlier, I had been her complete source of joy. I could do no wrong. But now, I was the enemy, and though I had carefully explained everything, her little mind was incapable of processing the information. She was unable to comprehend the bigger picture or the far better plan I had for her. All she knew was that she was not getting what she wanted when she wanted it, and nothing else mattered.

Is the emotional doubt that comes from our disillusionment with God much different? When He makes us wait or has something else in mind, do we throw ourselves to the floor and accuse Him of being unfair? With our inability to grasp the bigger picture, do we begin to doubt His involvement, His goodness, or even His existence? Do we cast all sorts of aspersions on His character simply because we want our pink jellies and we want them now?

Deuteronomy 29:29 says, "The secret things belong to the LORD our God, but the things revealed belong to us and to our children." Not only are we not in charge but we are incapable of that position. And, truth be known, we really wouldn't want it any other way. As someone aptly put it, if God were small enough for us to understand, He would not be large enough for us to worship.

Isaiah reminds us of our place before the God whose thoughts are far above man's thoughts and whose ways are far above man's ways (see Isa. 55:8). The apostle Paul builds on this: "Oh, the depth of the riches of the wisdom and knowledge of God! How unsearchable his judgments, and his paths beyond tracing out!" (Rom. 11:33).

Every time we take issue with God and begin to doubt His ability to handle things fairly, we're thrown into emotional turmoil and our faith begins to wane. When a person is not healed, a job not spared, or a marriage not saved, we begin to contemplate how we would do things differently if we were in charge. And that's the precise moment disillusionment and doubt, slowly and insidiously, begin chipping away at our faith.

We were created to live, to build, and to achieve. But if our faith is misplaced, or we don't allow for the fact that God may desire to achieve something special through the process, which may include a season of struggle, our worlds will be rocked every time we face the stark reality of our limitations.

Whether we admit it or not, most of us want to control, manipulate, or change every circumstance to make our lives what we think they should be. And while I would always applaud human effort, I also see how not recognizing and accepting our limitations can destroy us. Most people think that pride comes only when we feel superior to others, but pride is also our inability to see our limitations, admit our failures, or receive the help we need. Perhaps this is why Scripture so highly esteems a humble heart.

Humility vs. Pride

Humility is having a realistic idea of who we are, what we know, and what we're capable of. I'm convinced that the strength of our faith will always be in direct proportion to humility—a foundational truth that's missed by every atheist. The Old Testament prophet Micah, who was a contemporary of Isaiah and considered a minor prophet, made a major contribution by clarifying this truth better than anyone else in Scripture: "He has shown you, O mortal, what is good. And what does the LORD require of you? To act justly and to love mercy and to walk humbly with your God" (Mic. 6:8).

True humility pierces through the deep veneer of our delicate and prideful facade. It makes it nearly impossible to build the faulty logic that creates disillusionment and doubt. Sometimes our pride is challenged in monumental ways, other times through humorous ones. Years ago, coming home from our respective speaking engagements in different parts of the country, Jill Briscoe and I ran into each other at an airport. She told me that the airline had lost her luggage two days before, and she had worn the same outfit all weekend. After speaking for the third time in the same clothes, a woman from the audience waited in line to speak to Jill, then commended her for not trying to impress the audience with celebrity-like wardrobe changes.

The best model of humility, of course, the genuine article that we are to emulate, is the Lord Jesus Christ Himself, "who, being in very nature God, did not consider equality with God something to be used to his own advantage; rather, he made himself nothing by taking the very nature of a servant, being made in human likeness. And being found in appearance as a man, he humbled himself by becoming obedient to death—even death on a cross!" (Phil. 2:6–8).

Notice God the Father's response to God the Son's humble posture.

> Therefore God exalted him to the highest place and gave him
> the name that is above every name, that at the name of Jesus
> every knee should bow, in heaven and on earth and under the
> earth, and every tongue acknowledge that Jesus Christ is Lord,
> to the glory of God the Father. (Phil. 2:9–11)

I saw a great example of this posture of humility on *Larry King Live*
when pastor Greg Laurie was asked if believing in Christ was simply a
crutch. Pastor Laurie shook his head and replied, "No. Christ is not a
crutch. He is an entire hospital."

Peter said, "Humble yourselves, therefore, under God's mighty hand,
that he may lift you up in due time" (1 Peter 5:6). Dallas Theological
Seminary professor Howard Hendricks used to say, "The only way up
is down," and while this may sound counterintuitive or oversimplis-
tic, it is a deep and abiding spiritual truth. Faith cannot grow without
humility. Humility is the moist soil where faith takes root and intimacy
with God flourishes. It's the most important posture we can have as
Christians. I was reminded of this several years ago as I prepared to fly
home from a conference on the East Coast. I closed my suitcase and set
it by the door. I needed to hurry because I had one more session before
being driven back to the airport.

The weekend had been a great success, and I'd enjoyed speaking to a
diverse group of women. Now, they were gathering together for a final
time of worship. When I arrived at the session, I saw that the service
had already begun. The atmosphere was quiet and reverent as women
sang, shared thoughts on Scripture, and prayed together. There was also
a unique feeling to the weekend because many of the women at this particular conference had come from religious traditions that didn't allow
them to speak in front of their congregations or even attend church
without covering their heads.

Now, many of the younger women who had grown up in these churches were beginning to challenge some of the long-held traditions. I had the honor of mediating one of the open forums that weekend where the issues were freely discussed. It was refreshing to see women of such diverse opinions talk about sensitive issues with kindness and respect. I knew this morning session was special . . . especially for the older women who now stood up to speak freely.

The session was in full swing by the time I entered the building, so I quietly slipped in the back and found an empty seat. Just then, another latecomer came bustling in behind me, but clearly she was not as concerned as I was about the quiet reverence. She clumsily sat down next to me and began digging in a crinkly shopping bag she'd been carrying with her. Several eyes looked her direction with obvious disapproval, but she remained undeterred in her pursuit. Finally, she pulled something out of her bag. It was a crumpled, unused Kleenex. She carefully laid it on her lap, smoothed out the edges and gently placed it on top of her head. Then, she opened her hymnal and joined the rest of the women who had now begun to sing.

As I flew home that day, the Kleenex Lady kept coming to mind. I couldn't have imagined what was so important to her in that moment as I played both judge and jury to her noises. But she was the picture of humility in that place of worship. She was a woman who took seriously the honor and privilege of standing before a holy God; and though this wasn't my style of worship, her posture before the Lord was something worth emulating. It's the kind of posture where faith flourishes. Humility is the posture that lets us let someone else be right or be first. It's the kind of turn-your-cheek attitude that helps us to give blessings in the face of insults (1 Peter 3:9). It's the idea that God is God and I am not. Struggling for control is not a new concept. The apostle Paul gave an impassioned plea for the Romans to understand our place before God: "But who are you, a human being, to talk back to God? 'Shall what is formed say to the one who formed it, "Why did you make me like this?"'" (Rom. 9:20).

As far as I'm concerned, the best part about watching *Mr. Rogers' Neighborhood* was when Trolley took us to various manufacturers where we could see how pencils, work boots, or candy bars were made. One day, I saw a potter working at his wheel. The beauty of the pottery wheel, I soon realized, was that if the potter was displeased with the form his clay was taking, he could simply smash it down, smooth out the defects, and build it back up again.

Sometimes the defects were so small and inconsequential that Mr. Rogers was startled as the potter looked to be committing an act of violence against his art. Yet the imperfections were visible to the potter's eye and, of course, that's what mattered most.

Let's not dance around the obvious and deny God's involvement in the difficult times that come into our lives. Let's not allow such knowledge to disillusion us. Instead, let's dare to take everything a step further and find immense comfort in the fact that when the Potter presses out the clay of our lives, He is correcting imperfections and will surely craft us into things of beauty. Paul went on to say, "Being confident of this, that he who began a good work in you will carry it on to completion until the day of Christ Jesus" (Phil. 1:6).

Looking Deeper

1. When has disillusionment turned to doubt in your life?
2. What troubles you most about your faith?
3. How should doubt and disillusionment be addressed?

Chapter 12

FUELING THE FLAMES WITH ANXIETY AND DEPRESSION

When considering the emotional side of doubt, it's crucial to understand how feelings fuel our struggle, particularly with regard to anxiety and depression. Over a decade of speaking on a wide range of topics has convinced me that certain struggles are universal. Doubt is one of them, but closely linked are its companions, anxiety and depression. Combined, these topics generate the greatest response when I speak.

Many people are impacted by anxiety and depression—whether they receive help or not—at some point in their lives. The US Census Bureau conservatively reports that as of 2013, approximately three hundred million people live in the United States.[1] According to the National Institute of Mental Health, it is estimated that up to forty million of them will be affected by anxiety disorders, and another twenty million will struggle with depression.[2]

Anxiety and depression are huge obstacles for anyone to face, but they become particularly challenging for people who are trying to live by faith. Those who endure the personal struggle of mental illness, are often made to feel like second-class citizens in the church. Directly or indirectly, they're left feeling that if they'd just buck up under pressure or have more faith, they wouldn't have such problems. These kinds of messages are more than unhelpful; they are incredibly hostile. People

115

who battle clinical depression do not simply have the blues, nor do they need the added guilt that comes from thinking they've caused their illness or are hindering its cure. Often those with clinical depression and other mental disorders are suffering from a chemical imbalance. As research continues, doctors are better able to understand brain function and how illness impacts it. But any attempt to "help" the sufferer by suggesting they "toughen up" will only make their lives more difficult and cause them more reason to distrust God and His church. And if you have been on the receiving end of well-meaning believers whose uninformed and hurtful comments have wounded you the way they have me, please know that the God who knit you together in your mother's womb knows exactly what is happening inside your body and mind. He understands and accepts you as you are and invites you to allow Him to meet you exactly where you are.

The fact that I didn't suffer in silence is probably what saved me. My older brother, on the other hand, who suffered the same malady as I, kept his anxiety under wraps. As a result, his suffering became much worse. Six years my senior, he and I had bonded through music by the time I was in second grade, regularly helping myself to his records. If I returned them to him with a scratch, he never yelled. In fact, he celebrated our connection by taking me to a Moody Blues concert with his friends when I was thirteen. Even today, every time I play the Moody Blues, Cream, or the Kinks, I'm reminded of the bond that was a foreshadowing of the struggle we'd share.

My brother began struggling with panic attacks soon after graduating from college. The misdiagnosis of several doctors left him feeling the way I had—that somehow he was weak and bringing everything on himself. Through the years, my parents wondered what was wrong as they watched him move through jobs and relationships, often retreating as a complete recluse. He was with us the day I shared with my family the news of my recent visit to an internist, and how he had diagnosed and was treating my condition. It was a watershed moment when the light went on and my brother took me aside to say, "I think I have what you have."

There is a shame that surrounds mental illness that's complicated by sheer ignorance. But mental illness, which is often the product of physical illness, is not the result of weakness, lack of intelligence, or lack of faith. The extreme story of John Nash, popularized by one of my favorite movies, *A Beautiful Mind*, clearly illustrates that. In 1994, the professor became a Nobel Prize winner for economic excellence while battling schizophrenia. His brain was both brilliant and diseased.

During my panic disorder, I learned how to stay fit and live rightly. These life skills helped me reach my potential during my struggle, and became healthy lifelong habits. Yet, no matter how diligent I was about my behaviors, my anxiety was fueled by a physical problem, and it wasn't until I understood that fact that a medical solution was found. It's too easy for those who've never struggled with anxiety, depression, OCD, and the like to pass judgment on those who do. Even I used to wonder how anyone could feel desperate enough to self-medicate or hopeless enough to end their own life. I don't wonder anymore.

Anxiety can become oppressive in a variety of ways. Its unexpected forms can cause us to see things, hear things, feel things, and ultimately believe things that are just not real. Those of us who struggle with anxiety disorders—including obsessions, compulsions, panic attacks, or hypochondriasis—have lots of strange stories to tell . . . more than we would care to.

Disturbing thoughts that are generated by unhealthy brain function can be the source of tremendous doubt. The thin line that slices through thoughts and feelings is where emotions set up residence. But where one ends and the other begins is mysterious terrain indeed, and precisely what makes mental illness so troubling.

Rick and Kay Warren of Saddleback Church were committed to honoring their son's privacy as he battled mental illness, specifically clinical depression. When Matthew tragically ended his own life, the Warrens went public and became committed to educating the church, lest those who are struggling be held captive by ignorance and judgmentalism. Thrust into the limelight, the Warrens have been refreshingly candid.

Depression, even its mildest form, can keep us spiraling through a constant haze of cynicism and skepticism. Nothing feels quite right or real in our lives, including God, and rational thoughts become severely compromised.

Getting Healthy Enough to Combat Emotional Doubt

Struggling for more than a decade with panic attacks wreaked havoc on my emotions and made every one of my doubts much worse. It also made me more of an expert on anxiety than I ever wanted to be. I was desperate for answers and pursued every available source of information I could lay my hands on, including books, articles, interviews, and lectures. I may not be qualified to write an academic journal, but I've soldiered through stacks of them. My manic need for answers kept me tirelessly sifting through material, even past the point of exhaustion. One of the reasons I wrote this book was make all the information I gleaned through countless hours of research into something accessible.

Not only did I need to know what was causing my panic attacks, I needed to know how to make them stop. Until that happened, I found myself moving into survival mode. As a result, I developed an approach to health that served me well for the thirteen years of my panic disorder, and even now continues to be an important part of my life.

The first thing I discovered about maintaining healthy emotions, particularly under pressure, is that the body, the mind, and the spirit each demand their fair share of attention. Ignoring any one of them will only make matters worse. In fact, the first step toward diagnosing and treating any mental health problem is finding a qualified physician to examine your body. This needs to be someone you're able to communicate with, which can sometimes be trickier than we think. Take, for example, the term *panic attack* and how easily that's misinterpreted. For many, it's become a euphemism, simply a way to express feeling stressed out.

Also, I've noticed that when a physician is unable to immediately pinpoint the cause of a problem, many of them find it easier and perhaps less damaging to their professional ego to minimize the problem or shift the blame. Routinely, I'd hear things like, "There's nothing wrong with you. You just need to learn how to relax."

Learning how to relax is a great life skill. Finding healthy diversion in a project, particularly one that will benefit someone else, is immensely edifying. To some, being occupied with a hobby may seem frivolous, but there are times when it can be intensely beneficial to damaged emotions. My husband isn't nearly as prone to worry as I am, and though part of that was born into his nature, he also keeps himself busy. I suspect his building and repair skills, ones that could rival almost any professional, may also be the secret to his emotional health. Perhaps there is more to spackling than meets the eye.

Simply practicing the art of deep breathing can be helpful too. When we were kids and not feeling well at bedtime, my mom, who was way ahead of the yogis, routinely instructed us to roll over and take deep cleansing breaths. The relaxation that can be achieved through the discipline of deep breathing is both stress relieving and calm inducing.

The moment we step into a doctor's office, though, it doesn't matter what the problem is; we need someone who will both validate that problem, and try to fix it. Our society is high-strung, and in terms of survival skills, relaxation is vital, but learning to handle stress better didn't cure the source of my problem. The amazing doctor who finally diagnosed and treated my disorder took the approach any doctor worth his salt should take. *You're here. You're hurting. Let's not give up until we find a way to fix that.* How refreshing.

Once we've found a doctor we can communicate with, one who will take us seriously, a thorough exam needs to be done in order to rule out any underlying medical issues. Statistically speaking, most of our emotional suffering has a strong physiological component. Former first lady Rosalynn Carter has championed the cause of mental health. In her books and lectures, she has fought to eliminate the stigma attached to mental illness by bringing attention to the fact that far more often than not there is a medical basis for it.

Panic attacks and anxiety disorders have a plethora of physical components attached to them, including genetic predispositions, unhealthy brain function, and head trauma. Hyperthyroidism and hypoglycemia have also been linked to adrenaline problems that can cause acute anxiety. Medicine withdrawal is a major contributor, as is the use of stimulants including amphetamines, cocaine, and caffeine.

Depression can have strong physiological components attached to it as well. In fact, most cases of clinical depression are shown to be the direct result of chemical imbalances, which is why so many of them respond well to medication. Chemicals that carry signals to the brain—or neurotransmitters—can become out of balance as the result of illness, stress, trauma, or even genetics.

People who struggle with anxiety and/or depression should also examine their lifestyle choices. Day-to-day decisions we make may seem insignificant at the time, but they can have a powerful impact on our health. Often problems can be reduced or even eliminated through changes in diet or by physical activity. For example, aerobic exercise has been proven to provide the same mood altering endorphins, or "pleasure hormones," the body becomes robbed of through severe stress.

Technology has made it possible for people to work for hours without moving their bodies, but it was good old-fashioned hard work back on the farm that kept my ancestors healthy. They ate red meat, butter, and cheese, yet most of them lived well into their eighties and nineties. I wonder what my grandparents would think if they saw the rows of treadmills being used at my gym. To them it would seem an incredible waste of energy. To us, it's powerful medicine.

I became a runner during the years of my panic disorder primarily to release built up stress. A toned body was a pleasant by-product. The natural endorphins that are released in the brain during physical activity are almost as important as any other nutrient. Everyone can do *something*. Just move, even when your mind tells you not to. The best-kept secret is that regular exercise produces energy.

Our physical bodies, flawed as they may be, are remarkable pieces of machinery. They eat, sleep, digest, and reproduce. The fuel they take in can either keep them running smoothly or throw them off balance. For example, foods that are high on the glycemic chart, such as processed flour and sugar, can cause spikes and drops in insulin levels. This, in turn, impacts our immune systems, our energy levels, our sleep patterns, and even our ability to concentrate. Our entire nervous system is affected.

Instinctively, I knew that eating nutritious food was important during my panic disorder, though eating often became challenging. Intense anxiety often left me with no appetite and made simple body functions, such as swallowing food, almost impossible.

Along with regular exercise and proper diet, the restorative qualitiy of sleep helps strengthen the immune system, which can become deeply compromised through extreme stress. Most people need seven to nine hours of sleep a night, but for those who have anxiety disorders, sleep becomes even more important, albeit harder to get. Under the careful supervision of an internist, I found medication, combined with healthy sleep habits, to be the perfect way to achieve proper rest.

The Medication Debate

Some people, yes, even people of faith, will need to take medication; some for a while and others for life. Still, by now, I've heard just about every excuse there is for *not* taking it. Some refuse medication because they think it shows a lack of faith in God. Others fear the side effects they may experience. Still others avoid it altogether because of the stigma attached to it; they see medication as a sign of weakness.

I'll admit that as a culture we probably are overmedicated, mainly because we like a quick fix. Personally, I'm against taking meds simply to anesthetize our real issues. And I suppose an argument could be made for times of suffering. It has been known to build character, motivate change, and launch creativity. In fact, much of the art we enjoy is the direct result of someone's pain. What would the artistic landscape look like had artists such as Van Gogh, Mozart, or Hemingway been given antidepressants? The first strains of Brahms's Requiem are haunting and leave us breathless because they are encased by grief. Each of these artists has enriched our lives, but each paid an enormous price with their pain.

Also, I'm aware that the pharmaceutical world is big, big business. All we need to do is sit through one evening of commercials during *World News Tonight* to be reminded of that. We're given the impression that every problem known to mankind can be solved with a pill . . . though it may cause dry mouth, constipation, nausea, diarrhea, vomiting, dizziness, irritability, migraines, or an erection that lasts for more than four hours.

The really bad news of living in an overmedicated society is for those who genuinely need to be on meds. A knee-jerk reaction to all this pill popping can cause us to take a stand against any use of it. Magnify this a thousand times over for people in the church.

Doubt often plagues people who could physically and emotionally benefit from the careful and thoughtful use of pharmaceuticals. There are times when medication is exactly what is needed to make a difficult situation better, yet concerns do exist on this path to healing. I encounter three common objections.

1. The use of medication shows a lack of faith.

Theologically speaking, the possibility of both good and evil was introduced by God. The Bible points out that humanity's rebellion wreaked havoc on all of creation, which is why we need the work of redemption. The book of Romans says that Christ came to earth to restore it and to right its wrongs. Whereas His work on the cross paid in full the penalty for our sin—He paid a debt He did not owe, because we owed a debt we could not pay—He instructed us to continue on in the redemptive process. We're told to feed the hungry, visit the prisoner, and bind up the wounds of the sick. This "binding up" process often involves medical treatment, even as it did in Jesus' day. Genuine faith allows God to provide us with what we need to be the best we can be, whether it involves surgery, therapy, and/or medication. A case could be made that *not* making use of these resources is irresponsible and wrong. God can, and often does, bring healing through modern medicine.

2. All medicines cause side effects.

It's true that everyone responds to medication differently, and some will experience unpleasant side effects. However, I remind people that within the last decade alone there have been dozens of new medications that have come on the market. It's up to us to be our own best health advocate. If one medication doesn't work, we may need to try another. Finding the right solution to any health problem—the right doctor, the right meds, the right dosage—takes perseverance. It may also involve several attempts, but we can't give up. Eventually relief will come, and it will be well worth the effort.

3. Taking medicine is a sign of weakness.

The stigma traditionally attached to taking meds was undoubtedly born out of ignorance. It's extremely difficult to explain to someone who's never had clinical depression, acute anxiety, or an addiction just how out of control these struggles can be. The brain is an organ, like a kidney, and like other organs in the body, it can get sick. For example, mitral valve prolapse can cause the automatic response mechanisms in the brain to misfire or cut out altogether, which is called dysautonomia. Adrenaline is a good thing when we're competing in the Olympics or rescuing someone from a burning building, but when it kicks in at inappropriate times, such as during sleep or while quietly reading, as it did for me, it can be both frustrating and frightening. Taking meds to treat anxiety or depression can be as necessary as taking meds to treat kidney disease or diabetes. Over the years I've spoken to several families where the kids should have been put on medication but their parents saw meds as a weakness. Without the necessary medication, the kids sought relief the only way they knew how: through self-medication. Many of them have been in and out of rehab ever since.

In order to deal effectively with emotional doubt, we need to get a handle on our emotions. This may involve the counsel of a friend, a pastor, or a good therapist who can help us talk through disturbing thoughts and painful wounds. Or getting a handle on emotions may involve medication in order to relieve underlying medical issues that are fueling our distress. Learning how to slice through thoughts and feelings can prepare us to take the next step in our journey to overcoming emotional doubt.

Looking Deeper

1.   When is mental illness difficult to diagnose?
2.   How has anxiety or depression impacted your faith?
3.   What steps can be taken to alleviate anxiety and depression?

Chapter 13

CHANGING THE WAY
WE THINK

For thousands of years, philosophers have tried to grasp what the non-material dimension of our minds really is. It isn't enough to say that our thoughts are simply chemical reactions or electrical charges that the physical organ called the brain sets off. Nor is it enough to say that our thoughts are purely emotional reactions that function independently of our physical bodies. As is true with many subjects, the answer can be found somewhere in between.

The brain is a functioning organ that, when running smoothly, keeps the body clicking on all cylinders. However, like any other organ in the body, the brain can become sick or damaged. As a result, it can begin sending inaccurate messages to various parts of the body as well as troubling thoughts to the mind. For the one who is struggling with emotional doubt and trying to "live by faith," separating *intentional* thoughts from *unintentional* thoughts becomes extremely important.

Intentional Thinking

Anyone who struggles with mental illness knows how difficult it can be to control thoughts. Sigmund Freud, the father of psychoanalysis, divided the mind into two categories: the conscious and the unconscious. The conscious mind refers to everything we are aware of and intentionally make ourselves think about. The unconscious mind refers to everything we think about unintentionally, including things we may not want to think about. So intentional thinking is purposefully bringing to mind thoughts that would otherwise not likely show up.

Building on this premise, general practitioner and researcher Dr. Claire Weekes wrote what continues to be one of the most user-friendly books I've ever read on the topic of anxiety. She was a bit of a groundbreaker almost a half century ago and, in *Hope and Help for Your Nerves*, Dr. Weekes points out the direct correlation between how we think and how we feel, particularly as it relates to what she calls "nervous suffering."[1] As a Christian struggling with doubts that were intensified by damaged emotions, I found this to be immensely liberating.

Through a combination of fatigue, stress, fear, and adrenaline, people become "over-sensitized" to their emotions and vulnerable to negative thought patterns that unintentionally creep in. Dr. Weekes believes we can unlearn the bad mental habits that have taken root, and we can begin to reprogram our thought life through intentional thinking—which, by the way, is also a highly biblical concept.

The apostle Paul had a great deal to say about the mind and the discipline of intentional thinking. He warned us not to be conformed to the negative patterns of this world, but rather to become intentional by *renewing* our minds (Rom. 12:2), *dwelling* on what is true, noble, and pure (Phil. 4:8), and *taking* each thought captive and *making* each thought obedient to the One who promotes life to its fullest (2 Cor. 10:5).

Paul's choice of words shows deliberate action on our part, but sifting through thoughts and experiences that contribute to emotional doubt isn't easy. Soul searching requires a kind of stamina that's not for the faint of heart. After my venom was spewed on the day I lost my pregnancy, I remember sitting for a long time in silence. Then, ever so gently, God's Spirit began to speak to mine with Scripture I had "intentionally" committed to memory years before, beginning with, "Be still, and know that I am God" (Ps. 46:10).

In my emotionally stronger moments, I had committed to memory a lot of Scripture. In fact, as a child at youth group, we memorized verses, which at the time seemed to be for no other good reason than to earn a candy bar. Skeptics may accuse my guardians of having brainwashed me or having manipulated my worldview as a child, but don't be fooled. The atheist embraces and most certainly dispenses his worldview too. All I know is that in that painful moment, instead of wanting to die, rich spiritual truths came flooding back, assuring me that God was there and at work on my behalf, even in the midst of my sorrow. Intentional thinking is a discipline worth cultivating, if we want to rein in our emotions.

Unintentional Thinking

Unintentional thinking is allowing thoughts to pop in and out of our heads without effort or direction. Unlike Freud's free association—where the counselor encourages a patient to face thoughts and events that may be repressed—left to itself, an undisciplined or undirected thought life will steer an anxious person right off a cliff. Disturbing and painful thoughts become even more deeply embedded when we're fearful or fatigued—which is exactly what we are when we're in the midst of anxiety, depression, and doubt.

Anxiety can cause us to give more credit to disturbing thoughts than they deserve. Downplaying the negative thoughts and deliberately replacing them with better thoughts will help develop healthier mental habits that will eventually become second nature, just as the apostle Paul instructs.

Fleeting thoughts are random and pop into our heads for no specific reason. Most of them are hardly worth analyzing, but if we're wondering whether a thought is worth our focus and energy, the apostle Paul leaves us with the perfect litmus test: "Whatever is true, whatever is noble, whatever is right, whatever is pure, whatever is lovely, whatever is admirable—if anything is excellent or praiseworthy—think about [concentrate or dwell on] such things" (Phil. 4:8).

Over the years, a lot of books have been written on the topic of the mind and how we can think ourselves into and out of happiness or good health. Mind science gurus and metaphysical teachers have made their way onto cable channels and the talk show circuit a lot like faith healers who make their millions by convincing people they can heal their diseases through their mind-set, though there is very little science to back their claims.

That said, positive thinking can be an extension of intentional thinking and is always a good practice. I like to surround myself with positive thinkers in hopes that it might be catching. One of the trailblazers looking to conquer the topic of the mind's positive power was Dr. Norman Vincent Peale, who in the 1950s wrote *The Power of Positive Thinking*. It became an instant classic and shaped the attitudes of an entire generation. I devoured a copy of it myself decades later while in the throes of my own panic disorder and actually found much of what it had to say very helpful.

In his book, Dr. Peale points out the fact that bad thinking can become a bad habit. This, he states, will negatively impact not only our behaviors, but also our relationships, our jobs, our health, and our faith. According to Peale, we can create new habits and reeducate our minds by understanding how we got to where we are and by developing new thoughts that can propel us forward: "If your mind is obsessed with thoughts of insecurity and inadequacy it is, of course, due to the fact that such ideas have dominated your thinking over a long period of time. . . . Thought disciplining is required if you are to re-educate the mind and make it a power-producing plant."[2]

Crazy Thoughts

During my most severe bouts of anxiety and doubt, fearing I might be losing my mind, I started experiencing feelings of detachment or the sensation that I, or the world, didn't really exist. Much like déjà vu, also a sensation associated with emotions and moods, these feelings of being in an altered reality are much more penetrating and far more consuming. Nothing makes a sane person feel crazier than what experts refer to as *derealization*. Needless to say, it's awfully difficult to feel as though God is present when we don't feel present ourselves.

Many of the unhealthy thought patterns that keep a person ill are simply bad thoughts that have resulted from bad experiences. These kinds of disturbing thoughts need to be recognized, validated, and dealt with. However, more often than not, Weekes believes that many of our most troubling and obsessive thoughts are simply the result of harmless fleeting thoughts that have suddenly become wedged in our minds in a vulnerable moment, such as when we are frightened or fatigued.

It's only when a person understands the dynamics of fear—and how it takes hold of the mind and the body—that recovery can begin. Healthier minds produce healthier bodies, and to a large extent, we can impact both just by recognizing and understanding these dynamics.

It's easy to see how anxiety and depression can fuel our emotional doubts. Clearly, the body is impacted by mental illness, and mental illness is impacted by the body. The million-dollar question is which comes first: are emotional problems the result of physical problems, or do emotional problems cause physical problems? Sometimes the answer will be obvious, but other times, not so much. However, it's only when a person has dealt with the physical components of their situation that they'll have the strength they need to conquer the emotional.

Make Doubts Count

In order for us to take full advantage of our times of doubt and deal with them effectively, we first need to identify the kind of doubt we are facing, whether spiritual, intellectual, or emotional. Only then will we be able to come up with a practical plan of action that will allow us to benefit from those painful moments.

Spiritual doubt may require quiet introspection before God. It may warrant a few counseling sessions with a pastor, a professional, or a friend we can trust. Intellectual doubt may require a good fact-finding mission that can help us defend what we believe and why we believe it. Reading a few books on apologetics or taking a class can be extremely helpful. Emotional doubt is the hardest to recognize and the most troubling. However, it's only after our bodies and minds have been rested and restored through personal or professional attention that we can begin to think intentionally and to clearly separate facts from feelings and allow doubts to dissipate into faith.

Looking Deeper

1. Give an example of intentional and unintentional thinking in your own life.
2. How has emotional doubting impacted your relationship with God and with others?
3. What is the best way to take full advantage of emotional doubt?

PART THREE

Making Doubt Useful—Faith in the Real World

There are two ways to slide easily through life: Namely to believe everything, or to doubt everything; both ways save us from thinking.

Alfred Korzybski

Chapter 14

THE DAY I MET DOUBT

I was a junior at Northern Illinois University in the 1980s when I first noticed I had a problem. Looking back, there had been signs of trouble before that time, but it wasn't until a dreary January day that I realized something was seriously wrong. I had a strange feeling as I returned home from class that afternoon and was chilled to the bone. That wasn't unusual, though, as the cornfields of DeKalb do little to block the wind.

But this was different. I remember feeling slightly disoriented and nauseous as I stood in the kitchen, when suddenly a jolt of adrenaline shot through me. It gave me the sensation that something was crawling up and down the insides of my arms, my back, and my neck. I tried to lie down and calm myself, but I couldn't sit still. My heart was pounding as if I'd been running, and my breathing grew shallow. I felt powerless to stop myself from hyperventilation. I wasn't sure if I was having a heart attack or dying, but I was terrified.

Over the next several months each day got worse as the attacks became more frequent and, like any panic sufferer, I lived in constant fear, never knowing when the next one would hit. Not only were they becoming more intense, but they were incredibly random, sometimes even striking in my sleep. This made it impossible for me to see a pattern and figure out what could be triggering them. I was constantly on edge and at times my hands shook violently. Simple things like breathing

132

deeply or swallowing food became labored, and I was obsessed with checking my racing pulse.

It was clear that my body was reacting violently to something, but I couldn't nail down what it was. By the end of the semester I had developed enough avoidant behavior to keep me living in fear and phobias for the rest of my life. I had become a physical and emotional wreck.

There was also a deep sense of shame attached to my problem. I kept it secret, withdrew from all of my friends, and quietly struggled to get through my classes. I lived for the weekends, but not the way I used to. Friday no longer meant happy hour. It meant rescue. My dad would pick me up and drive me home where I could safely retreat. My parents did their best to comfort me with encouraging words, but in reality they knew even less about what was happening to me than I did. The part that really didn't make sense was *why* I was having what looked like a nervous breakdown. I hadn't suffered any trauma or abuse. I wasn't unhappy or under abnormal stress.

As the weeks and months passed by, I started making trips to the university health center hoping a doctor or counselor could fix me. But instead, I began hearing words that would be repeated many times in the years to come: "You're fine. You just need to learn how to relax." I learned very quickly that it can be true what people say about doctors, which is, when they don't know what else to call it, they call it *stress*. More than once I was sent on my way with relaxation tapes, vitamins, or valium.

I was frightened and frustrated and began obsessively searching the aisles of bookstores and libraries for answers. I read every health, mental health, and self-help journal I could find and became consumed with studies that dealt with psychoanalysis, behavioral therapy, post-traumatic stress disorder, bipolar disorder, and anorexia. All of them were legitimate causes for mental and emotional problems, and I desperately needed to find a clearly defined category that I could squeeze myself into. But I never could.

I read about repressed memory syndrome, which was trendy at the time, and because of its link to panic attacks, I decided to examine my own childhood for any hint of trauma or abuse. Maybe the problem was so deep, I couldn't see it. However, the more I dug, the more I realized what I already knew. My childhood wasn't perfect, but most of my memories were good. Old photographs evoked feelings of warmth and security. Home was a safe place filled with memories of summers spent with towheaded cousins on the shores of Lake Michigan. Sundays brought the stabilizing force of gathering for church, followed by chicken dinners and riding old bicycles our grandpa had rescued and restored.

I didn't know neglect, and I was untouched by divorce and dysfunction. Still, something was very wrong with me, and I was desperate for answers. I remained vigilant in my search, and because I was so desperate, no one was beyond suspicion, not even my family.

Eventually, though, my witch hunt came to an end, and again I was reminded of something I already knew. While some households hide deep secrets of alcohol and abuse, mine did not. The only thing I remember detecting on my parents' breath when they returned home from a night on the town with friends was Caesar salad. Hardly the stuff panic disorders are made of, but this knowledge only left me more confused than ever. I had nothing to blame my attacks on, so my search for answers continued with a mania that never seemed to tire no matter how exhausted I became.

With the absence of answers, my fear level increased, and I began to modify my behavior, which is the recipe for phobias. I avoided crowded spaces, caffeine, loud music, the evening news . . . anything that might upset me. I took up running and obsessed over what I ate, but while each solution brought a measure of comfort, relief was always fleeting. That's when I decided to look inside.

Six months earlier, life had been easy. It was all about designer jeans and frat parties. In fact, the only real problem I had with college was finding time for class. I'd been shallow and self-absorbed, hardly noticing the people around me. But now everything was different, and I became keenly aware of everyone, searching their eyes for signs that told me they might be searching too.

Finally, when no easy label could be stamped onto my physical, mental, or emotional suffering, my thoughts turned spiritual. They turned to God. I wondered if I'd offended Him or if He was punishing me for something. Was my problem guilt related? I compulsively searched for sins to confess and apologized to anyone who'd listen. Then, when even that didn't help, I started questioning Him. Doubts began to plow through me with a vengeance. I demanded to know where the loving God of my youth was in all of this mess. Did He really exist, and if so, why wasn't He helping me? The secure little evangelical world I'd grown up in suddenly made no sense.

Maybe I was possessed or losing my mind. For as long as I could remember I'd always believed in God, that He was good, and that He would care for me. Now I felt unsure of everything. In retrospect, the physical and emotional pain became nothing compared to the spiritual disillusionment.

One night I walked into the bathroom and saw in the mirror the mess I'd become. Thin and pale, I gripped the sides of the sink to steady myself, closed my eyes, and pleaded for help from a God I hoped was there. *Please, do not let me lose my mind.* There were no flashes of light in that moment and no instant cures. In fact, I felt no different as I walked back to my room that night. But in reality, that brief and sincere prayer set into motion things I couldn't see or even imagine at the time.

A New Start

In the days ahead, my panic attacks continued to randomly increase and decrease in severity. Over time, I learned how to take advantage of the moments when I felt stronger, working fast to get done as much as I could before the others would hit. Somehow I completed college, got my degree, and married a guy who stuck with me through the whole ordeal. And though full-time motherhood is a tremendous calling, I became the quintessential stay-at-home mom mainly out of fear of having a panic attack in public; I admired career women with their tailored suits and briefcases who were the confident picture of everything I wasn't.

When my husband's job relocated us to Milwaukee, I decided I would force myself to make a fresh start. I'd meet the women in my neighborhood, even if it killed me. I had heard about a group of women who met at a large church in the metropolitan area and eventually mustered the courage to check them out. At first, I snuck in and out unnoticed, always able to find the lone seat in the back. I wasn't sure what all I agreed with, but the tall, slender woman at the podium captivated me with her lilting British accent. She was insightful and articulate, and I listened carefully as she examined life with its challenges, on both a practical and a philosophical level. Her intellectual approach to faith allowed me to move outside the perimeter of my damaged emotions. My feelings and painful thoughts didn't need to dominate my life. They weren't the final authority.

Even her biblical references were relevant, and I found myself remembering dozens of verses I thought I'd forgotten. The texts began taking shape in my mind, adding substance and texture to my struggle. I knew I didn't have the strength or the wherewithal to conquer life on my own. A worldview was not going to be enough. I needed empowerment, and for the first time, I dared to consider the possibility that my suffering wasn't an accident . . . that it wasn't the result of personal weakness, sin, or a lack of self-control.

As the months went by, I felt myself changing. Physically I continued to struggle, but spiritually I began to thrive. One morning, after the group was dismissed and I was preparing to make one of my trademark exits, I was approached by the coordinator. She was in charge of the small group leaders, and after sitting in on our group discussion, she said she'd noticed me and wondered if I'd be interested in sharing some thoughts in front of the entire group the next Thursday. Nothing big, she said, ten minutes or so.

I stood frozen somewhere between shock and flattery. Then, before anyone could stop me, I heard myself saying I'd love to. But as I left the building and piled my books and kids into the minivan, I wondered what in the world I'd just done by agreeing to speak in front of a large crowd of women. Had I somehow forgotten I had panic attacks? And the fact that these attacks were intense and debilitating was nothing compared to the fact that they could strike at any moment without warning.

I had worked very hard at keeping my panic attacks a secret. And like all panic sufferers, I had become highly skilled as an escape artist. No matter where I ventured—grocery stores, shopping malls, or libraries—I always knew where every exit was at any given moment. Disappearing from a podium in front of two hundred pairs of eyes was bound to be trickier.

Arguing with God

For days I was in a kind of denial and spent hours preparing for a talk I knew I'd never give. Maybe I could pull it off, I told myself. Maybe no one would notice the sweating, the shaking, or the shortness of breath. But I knew that those things would be the least of my worries if I tried to walk on stage and take the microphone. I knew that the much bigger threat was fainting in front of hundreds of women or completely freaking out.

Still, I became consumed with those ten minutes that lay before me and continued preparing with a desire that was growing almost as strong as my fear. I wanted to tell the women what I was learning . . . that this world is a very troubled place, but we can take heart because Christ has overcome the world. God isn't good because He gives pay increases, safe travel, or clean bills of health. He is good because His nature demands it . . . even when we hurt and things don't make sense.

But as Thursday drew closer, my anxiety level was through the roof.

My talk was ready, but the fear of having a panic attack in front of an audience was almost unbearable. Even for the best of us, public speaking remains people's number one fear. Jerry Seinfeld once pointed out that death is the second, which means we're better off lying in the casket than having to give the eulogy.

The audience I'd be speaking to included a large number of women from the gray-haired set, and I had no desire to traumatize them or send them into cardiac arrest. I wanted to cancel in the worst way, but I knew it was too late . . . it was set . . . it was preordained . . . my name was already in the bulletin. So I began pleading with God to find me a way out, to send storms, floods, or pestilence . . . anything. But Thursday morning arrived, sunny and right on schedule.

Looking back, the night before I was to speak was pivotal with regard to the life God was preparing me for. It was very late when I walked downstairs and stood in the living room. The house was dark as I stood in the stillness. I was so frightened by what I was about to face the next morning, it was almost laughable. Yet, as I stood there, I remember having enormous resolve.

Then, suddenly, without visions, voices, or theatrics, I became keenly aware of the presence of evil. I'd never experienced anything like it, nor have I since, but in retrospect, I understand just what was at stake. I was about to be launched into an international speaking ministry that would touch thousands of lives. And while I may not be skilled to look into such things, if ever there seemed a good reason for good and evil to take issue with each other, this might have been one of them. I wasn't exactly sure who was listening, but in that moment I decided to make Job's words my own and said out loud, "Even if He slay me, I will hope in Him." That's when I knew just how it would go down. I wasn't sure of the details, but there'd be no retreating. Broken body, broken mind—it didn't matter. My spirit was strong.

I'd like to say I was miraculously healed overnight and ready to speak by morning, but I wasn't. In fact, I was a wreck and dreading the discomfort of standing in front of a crowd of people and making a fool of myself. But because obedience is not about looking good or feeling good, I picked up my notebook and headed for the front door.

Then, just as I was about to close it behind me, the phone rang, and I heard a woman's voice on the other end. She said we'd never met, but she knew who I was. She said she was on the prayer committee at church and had noticed my name in the bulletin. She'd been praying for me that morning and had a verse of Scripture she wanted to share with me. I was in a hurry, but I politely jotted it down and thanked her.

How nice, I thought, as I hurried back to the front door. I admired people who took prayer seriously. But as I stood in the doorway, I wondered if it might not be a good idea to take a moment and actually look at the words she'd given to me. My hands were a little unsteady as I flipped through the pages of my Bible to the book of Acts, and there I found her reference in the eighteenth chapter, verses 9 and 10. "Do not be afraid; keep on speaking, do not be silent. For I am with you."

I heard my talk went very well that morning. I don't remember a thing except being surrounded by several women when I finished, and being told I was gifted. I wept the entire ride home. Why does it have to be so hard, Lord?

When my husband came home from work that day, I was still crumpled and crying on the couch. Naturally he assumed the worst, but when I told him that not only had it gone well but the women said I was gifted, he smiled and asked, "And that's why you're crying?" His comment wasn't exactly what I was looking for, but I knew he cared. And, after all, when is it ever exactly what we're looking for? Like the time he stood by me in the delivery room, and after twelve hours of hard labor, turned to me and gently said, "You could use some gum."

This time, though, my husband was spot on, and I realized I was crying because there was nothing I wanted more than to be a speaker. But I also knew that would be out of the question. This was probably a

onetime deal, and like so many other experiences in my life, I'd probably never be able to do it again. *Oh ye of little faith . . .*

Then my husband suggested that maybe it was time to give one more
doctor a try. We both knew this was a sore subject, as doctors hadn't
been much help through the years, but I was desperate. So when he
suggested I visit the doctor he'd recently met, I agreed to make one
more appointment.

By the time I walked into Dr. Tim's office, I knew enough not to get
my hopes up again. In fact, I decided to take a different approach this
time and see if he was actually worth the rows of diplomas that hung on
his wall. I wouldn't tell him why I was there, other than for a checkup.
If he was good, he'd tell me.

We talked vaguely about health issues and family history as he examined me. He asked questions about nutrition, exercise, and lifestyle
choices. Then, it happened. As he spent what felt like an inordinate
amount of time listening to my heart, he asked if I'd ever been told I
had mitral valve prolapse. I told him I hadn't, as he continued to listen
through his stethoscope. He said he could hear the signature clicking
and that it was a fairly common disorder, typically not too serious. In
fact, some people don't even know they have it, he said, before moving
on. Then, almost as an afterthought, he added, "Sometimes people can
have bothersome symptoms, such as skipped heartbeats, a racing pulse,
headaches, or feelings of anxiety." He looked at me and asked, "Have
you ever had a panic attack?"

I was so shocked that for the first time in my life I was actually
speechless. But when I finally found my voice again, the floodgates
opened, and I couldn't get my words out fast enough. Between sobs, I
described the secret shame that had been my life for more than thirteen
years. He listened without interruption, the first sign of a really good
doctor, and politely handed me some tissues.

When I finally took a breath, he said that none of what I'd described
surprised him. He explained about the heart, the pulmonary system,

and how the adrenaline of mitral valve prolapse can take a propensity toward anxiety and multiply it several times over. It was a bit disquieting when he momentarily stepped out of the examining room and I saw my life reduced to two words scribbled on a notepad: *panic disorder*. But my doctor put me on heart medication that very day, and my thirteen-year nightmare came to an end.

Looking Deeper

1. When did you and doubt first meet?
2. Describe a time when you argued with God.
3. How do the body, mind, and spirit impact each other and our faith?

Chapter 15

Rethinking Doubt

People often ask me where I got my training as a speaker. They're waiting for me to tell them that I majored in communications on a full scholarship to some great university or that I enrolled in a fabulous public-speaking program. But the truth isn't nearly that glamorous. In fact, the only speech classes I ever had were the ones required of every college freshman at Northern Illinois University, which fortunately were prior to the full onslaught of my panic disorder. In high school, I stood up like everyone else and demonstrated how to make amazing brownies or persuaded classmates not to smoke. My grades were decent, but I was definitely no standout.

At the risk of sounding uber-spiritual, when people ask me where I got my training, I tell them it was out in the desert with Moses . . . circling, but never quite reaching the Promised Land. When you consider that it took the Israelites forty years to make what should have been a three-week trek, you have to ask yourself what in the world they were doing out there. How could they possibly have kept missing it?

From a human perspective they were absorbed in the monumental tasks of moving flocks and herds and people. We're also told in the Old Testament that they did a lot of complaining, which we know can be very time-consuming. But from God's perspective, it was His sovereign control that kept them from reaching the Promised Land until He decided the time was right.

Training in the Wilderness

Like the Israelites, my wilderness experience lasted a long time—too long from my perspective. I had struggled and searched for thirteen years and had covered countless miles. In the end, though, the doctor who gave me back my life had an office that was less than two miles from my home. How could *I* have kept missing it?

Scripture offers very little explanation about how our freedom of choice might work in light of God's sovereign control. The Old Testament book of Daniel, however, does give us an interesting glimpse.

As a young man, Daniel stood out from the crowd because of his good looks, his physical strength, and his intellect. When the kingdom of Judah was captured and Daniel was forced to serve the foreign king, he did what he could to cooperate during training. But when it came to compromising his standards, this impressive young man refused to break the dietary restrictions that were important to his Jewish faith. Daniel dared to challenge the official who had been put in charge of his food and drink.

In the first chapter of Daniel we read, "Daniel resolved not to defile himself with the royal food and wine, and he asked . . . for permission not to defile himself this way" (v. 8). The official in charge was nervous, though, and told Daniel that the king would have his head if he saw Daniel looking worse than the other prisoners. So Daniel told the official to test him and give him nothing but vegetables to eat and water to drink for ten days and see if he didn't look better than the others. After ten days, he did look better, so the official took away his choice food and wine and gave him water to drink and vegetables to eat instead.

What's noteworthy about this narrative is not only did it launch the successful "Daniel Diet," but it powerfully illustrates an enormous amount of self-control on Daniel's part. Choice food and wine from the king's table would have been the perfect escape for Daniel from such a dismal situation. And who would blame him?

However, what really catches my eye are the two words found in verses 8 and 9 that speak volumes of the balance between human responsibility and divine sovereignty. Daniel *resolved* not to defile himself, and God *caused* the official to show him favor.

I used to wonder how gymnasts learned to do their amazing routines on the balance beam. Most of us couldn't bend or bounce that way on the floor, let alone on a beam that's less than four inches wide. Then, when my daughter was very young, she took gymnastics for about three seconds, and I was able to learn the trick. The instructor lowered the beam all the way to the floor. Then she encouraged the leotard-clad four-year-olds to walk back and forth, and they did so without any fear of falling. As the students progressed and gained confidence, the beam was raised.

Scripture raises the beam for us, too, with regard to the weighty concept of divine sovereignty. As followers of Christ, if we want to grow and develop, we can expect to be stretched and challenged, which, as any Olympian would attest, won't be easy.

We may wish we had more options, but when the tough times come, we really only have two: turn toward God or turn away. I've done plenty of both, and I've discovered that turning away comes pretty easily when we're hurting, but it leaves a bitter aftertaste. Turning toward God might not come naturally in the beginning, but it's definitely a discipline worth cultivating because it provides not only a healing balm like nothing else can, but also an opportunity for our faith to be strengthened.

Occasionally, we hear about people who've spent decades in prison for crimes they didn't commit. I ran an Internet search on the names of two falsely accused men I recently heard about on the news because I was interested in hearing their stories in their own words. I was curious about any anger they might be harboring and how it might be impacting their lives. Certainly, each of them had the right to be angry, but I was amazed to find no visible signs of bitterness in either of them. In fact, both credited their faith in God for having gotten them through their nightmare, and they looked forward to the next chapter in their lives.

We may have no control over a difficulty that comes our way, but we do have something to say about how we respond, and this will look different for each one of us. Personally, when I'm hurt, I need to vent my displeasure to someone who'll listen. My family gives me that permission, and they supply the opportunity I need to process my pain and anger before I can turn it over to God. Sometimes we need a release—a cry, a run, a scream—before we can hand things over, but we'll know we're making progress as the time it takes to give it over gradually lessens. It might even take a few attempts before we can give something over completely, without snatching it back. But like the gymnast on the beam, repeated practice allows us to develop.

In the 2006 movie *Little Miss Sunshine*, a troubled teenage boy, who admires Nietzsche and takes a vow of silence, is consoled by his equally unhappy uncle. As the uncle gives a pep talk to the boy, and ultimately to himself, he points out the importance of learning and growing through painful experiences. He names several artists who did just that, then reminds the boy not to waste the angst-driven years of high school, as they are some of the best opportunities to suffer.

We'll all be given plenty of opportunities to turn away from God and become cynical, just as many of the Jews did on their difficult desert trek. One day, not long after my diagnosis, while discussing my wilderness wanderings with my dad, I lamented the time it took to find my answer when it was so close by.

My panic disorder robbed me of years that could have been spent in continued education, a career, or world travel. Instead, they were restricted in many ways, and I was defined by fear. After listening to my complaint, my dad reminded me of something I needed to hear. As with the Israelites, God knew when the time was right. God knew exactly when His people were ready to reach their destination, and He knew exactly when it was time for me to reach mine. He who wastes no time or teardrop was preparing me for something larger. What better way to be trained to rely on God than to have to spend forty years out in the desert with Moses?

I absolutely should not be a public speaker—I have a history of panic attacks, and the two do not go together. But somehow God provided me with a moment of clarity amidst my chaos, and I invited Him to take my despair and turn it into something fine. Daniel was thrust into a difficult situation as a captive in Babylon. From what we're told, he was a good Jewish boy minding his own business. He could have become mired in doubt and disillusionment, yet, when adversity struck, he chose to rise to the occasion, and God went on to use his life in powerful ways.

Every one of us is called to some sort of task or ministry in life, and it's incredibly liberating the moment we realize that not only will God set a goal for us, but He'll also empower us to achieve it, if we let Him. There are plenty of things God forces on us, but His empowering to achieve full success isn't one of them. The amazing irony of God's control and love is that it often doesn't feel as though He is in control or particularly loving. That's why God feels strangely absent in our struggles and doubts. How do we reconcile that God is good, has ultimate control, and loves us deeply, with the fact that He uses tragedy, doubt, and pain to help us? To our human minds, it would seem that doubt and pain would only bring more doubt and pain, and that adversity is evidence of the absence of God.

We struggle with the sovereignty of God—His right to do what He does because He is the supreme power—for basically two reasons. The first is because we can't understand how His sovereignty works, and the second is because, from our perspective, it often appears unfair. It's a concept that, as J. I. Packer puts it, "scandalizes our tidy minds."[1] We like things organized, like the magazines I stack neatly on my desk or the window shades I must draw to the exact same length. Anything less makes my brain feel lopsided . . . an idiosyncrasy my kids love messing with. They'll walk by my desk with a gleam in their eyes and gently push all of my magazines out of place, ever so slightly, then tell me it's for my own good. I try to explain that my magazines and window shades are the only things in life I can completely control; leave them alone.

Not only do we want our minds tidy, but we want our lives tidy too. We want balance and fairness. We're sure nothing would make us happier than living in a world where people actually get what they deserve. As Rob Bell often points out, we really don't want a God who doesn't judge. We want immediate judgment on every bad thing that happens. And we want that judgment to make sense to us. We want to believe that the parents of random shooters are monsters or that people get lung cancer because they smoke. However, when both ideas are sometimes proven to be untrue, our magazines and window shades get all jazzed up. It's an uncomfortable truth that leaves us feeling as though we need to apologize for God to a watching world—as though God needs defending. St. Teresa of Avila is credited as saying to God, "If this is the way you treat your friends, it's no wonder you have so few!"

When life feels so senseless and random, we struggle trying to process this side of God's nature. But if we can stretch ourselves to consider the possibility of a God who goes to tremendous lengths to allow us our independence, and yet desires us to desire Him, a different set of possibilities may open up to us and our perspectives may begin to change.

Every one of us will be given ample opportunity to get this right—to trust God and test our faith. This is not to say that things won't get messy. In fact, I'll admit that after all I've been through, when I hear people pray and use words like, "Lord, help me to grow" or "Whatever it takes, Lord," I have to fight the urge to gasp just a little and take a few steps back. *Move awaaaay from the praying zone.*

It's not that I don't believe great things will happen to the one who is doing that kind of praying. Indeed, I'm convinced they will. It's just that I also know it won't be quick, it won't be easy, and rarely will it be pain-free. God never promises an easy road this side of heaven. We need to get that straight.

Perhaps one day we can ask God why He designed life that way, but like every good parent, sometimes God reveals His love for us through unpopular decisions intended to help us reach our potential. And He does this without violating the delicate balance of human responsibility and divine sovereignty. Kids often view their parents as harsh buzzkills; we often view God the same way. We want to get where we need to go, but we want the path of least resistance to get there.

Sitting on a plane recently, waiting to pull away from the gate, I heard an announcement on the intercom. *Sorry folks. One of the engines won't start. Our mechanics will have to take a look.*

I heard a collective groan ripple through the seats as fingers flipped through smart phones and mental adjustments were made to accommodate the unwelcome news. Then, quite abruptly, the mood shifted. I could almost slice through the thick silence that pressed through the cabin as each of us sat wondering what the pilot could possibly say next that would convince us that staying on that plane was a good idea. *Don't worry, folks, we've fixed it? We got 'er started?*

Suddenly, there was stirring in the back of the plane, and I realized a passenger was having a panic attack. As his wife tried to calm him, I sat with my head back and my eyes closed, trying to remember how to breathe. I found myself drifting back fifteen years when I too had been crippled by panic attacks. I felt for the guy, but it was in that moment that I realized how far I had come. Not only was I in a stressful situation and not having a panic attack but I was able to respond with sympathy and even pray for the poor guy and his wife.

Most of us want God to make us better people, strengthen our faith, and even use us in some positive way. But how many of us truly consider what that will look like? We like the idea of being mature and complete and lacking in nothing, as James puts it, but we tend to gloss over what that will entail. Scripture, however, doesn't gloss over a thing.

> No discipline seems pleasant at the time, but painful. Later on, however, it produces a harvest of righteousness and peace for those who have been trained by it. Therefore, strengthen your feeble arms and weak knees. "Make level paths for your feet so that the lame may not be disabled, but rather healed." (Heb. 12:11–13)

Marathon runners don't begin their race at the starting line. They begin months earlier when they drag themselves out of bed and run their first lap around the block. By the time I sat buckled in my seat, waiting to hear from the pilot, I'd run quite a few of those spiritual laps. There have been no shortcuts to learning what it means to walk with a sovereign God. Learning to confidently pray for peace and the well-being of my family, should God choose to take me in that moment, didn't come overnight either. Again, it was a cultivated skill, a spiritual discipline that I will continue to work on until I stand in God's presence.

I'm happy to say I was ready that day, as I sat on the plane and waited. Though I will admit I was equally happy when the announcement was made that we would be boarding a new plane.

Our struggles with doubt can become amazing opportunities for growth. We need not fear them nor should we waste them. Like it or not, and I'll be the first to admit I do not, trials become a part of the faith-building process by stretching the limits of pure autonomy. From the moment I first heard the oft-quoted, "God cannot use a man fully until He has wounded him deeply," I had issues with it. Eventually, however, I learned that for reasons known only to Him, this is the way

God set up this autonomous world. He often tears us down before He builds us back up, and while this may be an absolute gateway to glory, it doesn't mean we'll always like it.

Displeasure does not always equate to doubt, though. I've come to realize that my faith in God hasn't waned nearly as often as I've struggled with His plans. Just because we get frustrated with God's plan doesn't mean that we are doubting our faith.

Without the possibility of a God who ordains both pleasure and pain and who not only works in the midst of our mess but can control it, our lives can begin to take on the qualities of hopelessness, futility, and despair. But by rethinking doubt and God's willingness to use it to strengthen our faith, we open ourselves up to all sorts of amazing opportunities.

As ironic as it sounds, those who are confronted with the greatest difficulties in life and find a way to accept God's plan, are the ones for whom God feels more fully present in their lives. In 1 Peter 3:12, Peter tells believers that when they suffer and choose to do the righteous thing, the eyes of the Lord are on them and His ears are especially attentive to their prayers.

Recently, I was reminded of this when I pulled out my middle-school yearbook from back in the days when it was called "junior high." As I started thumbing through pages that looked like something straight out of *That '70s Show*, I was amazed by the number of faces that still seemed familiar to me after all these years.

As I began wondering what happened to everyone, I came across a snapshot of the teachers and their spouses who had chaperoned the eighth-grade trip to Washington, DC. I'd seen the picture many times before, but suddenly it felt as though I were looking at it for the first time. The row of teachers who'd seemed ancient to me years ago now looked very young. Their fresh faces told the story of kids straight out of college. For most of them, this was their first real job.

One of the faces that caught my attention was that of Coach Willis. As a teacher at Batavia Junior High School, Scott Willis had been a favorite. With his long blond hair and wire-rimmed glasses, we thought him a dead ringer for John Denver. As I studied his picture, I remembered his kindness. He taught kids with extra needs, coached the junior high wrestling team, and was rarely alone. Kids loved him and flocked around him. He traveled in packs.

As he stood beside his wife, smiling at the camera, with his promising future stretched out before him, no one could have imagined the horror that lay ahead. Almost twenty years later, I was at home in Milwaukee watching the news when I heard about a horrific accident that had just taken place on a local highway. A semi had dropped some debris on the road, and a white minivan carrying a family had run over it, causing the gas tank to spark and catch fire. Within seconds, the entire vehicle was engulfed in flames as two parents burned their flesh in a frantic attempt to rescue their children. In the end, they were helpless and saw five of their children perish before their eyes. As I watched the story unfold on the news that day, I was overwhelmed with grief. But it wasn't until that evening that the event hit much closer to home. My sister called and asked if I recognized the names of the victims in the accident. I told her I didn't. Then she said it was Coach Willis from Batavia Junior High and his family.

Over the next several days and weeks, I was glued to the modern-day Job story. I watched as the grief-stricken parents tried to process what had happened. At times they wept openly, but at other times they seemed strangely composed. I saw them struggle to explain their faith and the strength they drew from the knowledge that one day they would be reunited with their family in the presence of God. The media didn't know what to make of the Willis family and insisted they must be in denial, because although it was obvious their grief was tangible, it was also obvious they weren't grieving like those who have no hope (see 1 Thess. 4:13).

An older Willis child who lived outside of Milwaukee, the son the family was on its way to visit that dark day, was converged upon by the media. As they thrust their microphones in his face, waiting for a statement, through his grief he said softly, "The Lord giveth, the Lord taketh away. Blessed be the name of the Lord."

In the days ahead, I watched Coach Willis, who by then had become Pastor Willis, struggle to explain his faith to a watching world. The media puzzled as he spoke of his assurance that one day he would see his children again.

This kind of faith doesn't just slip into our lives without notice. More than a decade later, the Willis family has become a powerful witness to one unwavering truth: God gives more of Himself to those who give more of themselves to Him. They have done amazing work for the kingdom, all along keeping their eye on the prize. Whatever heaven looks like, one day Coach Willis will stand before the Lord with his children spread around him and hear the unfathomable words we'd all like to hear: "Well done, good and faithful servant."

God's Active Role

Is God sadistic, as skeptics accuse? Or is the unfathomable depth of man's freedom of choice sadistic? Would we be better off with less latitude? We seem to think so, at least when we are hurting. God promises to meet us at our greatest point of need and provide for us, whether through persons or circumstance, and He does so without violating the delicate balance of His sovereign control and man's free will. And while most of us will never be tested the way Scott Willis was, God will create opportunities for our faith to flourish wherever we're planted. He won't usurp our freedoms to trust Him, curse Him, or disregard Him completely, nor will He simply wind us up, pull the string, and sit back to watch us spin like a top. He strikes the perfect balance.

A few years ago, I was returning from a conference and found myself flipping through the radio dials on my long drive home. When I'd had enough jazz, classical, alternative, and oldies, I finally landed on NPR and caught the tail end of an interview.

A panel of journalists was discussing a documentary they'd filmed on poverty down in the Mississippi Delta. They'd followed the life of an African American woman who lived in a trailer with four or five kids. At one point, the woman was trying to scrape together enough money to buy her kids basic school supplies. She believed that education was their only way out.

Each journalist admitted how hard it was to film her struggle when what they really wanted to do was open their wallets. However, they explained that they couldn't intervene because this was a documentary. As one of them put it, "We are journalists. We're not in the business of changing reality. We film it."

As I drove along, I thought about the great weekend I'd just spent at the conference, speaking to hundreds of women. It had been a powerful time, a real shot in the arm for all of us. However, I'd reminded the women as we finished up our last session that soon we'd be climbing down from our mountaintop and heading back home. Things that had been left on Friday would still be there when we returned . . . in spades. Laundry baskets would be overflowing, dirty dishes stacked, and last-minute homework projects spread across dining room tables. And these, I reminded them, would be the easy things. Some would be returning to rebellious kids or husbands annoyed by yet another "religious" event. Some of them would be returning to houses that were too empty.

It would have been discouraging to think about, but as I crossed the Illinois state line I took pleasure in a different thought. It was comforting to realize that unlike the journalists, God would never say, "I'm not in the business of changing reality . . . I just film it." Sometimes it feels as though God winds things up and lets them go, but fortunately the truth of Scripture assures us that God is in the business of changing reality, and He begins by changing us. His compassions are new *every* morning (Lam. 3:22–23).

Everyone needs permission to dig deep and unearth the source of their doubt. It's only in retrospect that I now understand the pain that was ordained for me and why it took as long as it did to find the solution to my problem. I was in training, and so are you. Rest assured, God is involved in ways that may seem insignificant at the moment, but eventually we will be able to see the extraordinarily big picture.

I was reminded of this one day, quite a while after my panic disorder had come to an end. I asked my husband how he actually found the doctor who gave me my life back. Was it the result of his extensive research? Did he secure a great referral through his tireless quest?

We were living outside of Milwaukee at the time, and my husband, employed by Andersen Windows, needed to find a physician for routine checkups. One day, while driving near our home, he spotted a medical building that had been built with Andersen Windows. He parked his car, went inside, made an appointment, and the rest is history.

That was the day I realized that no detail is insignificant to God if it matters to us. Life is hard and difficult to sort out. No one would deny that. But I've seen firsthand how tiny measures of joy can slice through our pain and heighten our sense of God. They can propel us toward the ultimate goal of knowing Him better in our spirit, our body, and our mind.

So let's not waste questions that come and challenge our faith. Let's think them through carefully and ask God to give us an eternal perspective on our pain and a glimpse into the plans He might have for it—because, remember, those who've never really doubted have never *really* believed.

Looking Deeper

1. Why do we fear doubt?
2. Why is doubt hard to admit?
3. What is the best and worst way to make use of our times of doubt?

TEN REASONS NOT TO BE A CHRISTIAN

Doubt can be devastating, but it can also open up amazing opportunities for growth. The possibilities that surround the prospect of understanding ourselves and our God better are limitless. If this book has been able to communicate a little bit of that, it will have done its job.

Initially, I'd considered devoting the final section of this book to addressing tougher questions asked of the Christian faith. Some of the more common ones include, *If God is good, why is there suffering? What happens to people who don't know Jesus?* However, I've touched on many of them in the book, and these questions, and many more like them, have been masterfully addressed by some of the brightest, most enlightened minds on the planet, including William Lane Craig, Ravi Zacharias, John Lennox, and so on. (See suggested resources.)

Instead, I've taken a slightly different approach. After years of staying up too late and surfing the Net, I decided to address some of the criticisms leveled by skeptics who've posted comments following YouTube debates and online articles about atheism. (Yes, I read them.) Clearly, there are plenty of people who simply enjoy being difficult. I often sense this when I'm listening to atheists debate. Many of them are brilliant in so many ways that I deeply respect, but they become intentionally obtuse, blurring the religious lines between the likes of Osama bin

Laden and Mother Teresa. It's hard to take seriously those who resort to broad-brushing Christians by labeling them irrational bigots; though, there are probably plenty of believers who fall into that category. But Christians hardly have a corner on the idiot market. There is plenty of idiocy to go around.

Other posts, however, share honest concerns and express difficulties many have with religious people and with religion in general—many concerns I share myself. Even among professing Christians, misconceptions abound. So I thought I'd try to address a few objections to the Christian faith.

1. Faith in God Is Required for Happiness

One of the common Christian platitudes atheists and skeptics are offended by and react against is the statement that one cannot be happy, enjoy life, or even have a healthy relationship unless they have faith in God. This simply is not true. Look around. There are lots of nonbelievers who are happy and enjoy life with its many blessings—though they're more apt to say they've been lucky. Even Scripture points out the fact that common blessings are for the benefit of all people: "He causes his sun to rise on the evil and the good, and sends rain on the righteous and the unrighteous" (Matt. 5:45).

All people, including atheists, enjoy the blessings of God, whether they acknowledge Him or not. This is not to say that their lives couldn't be enhanced or taken to another level with greater insight from God—though with greater understanding comes greater accountability, but that's a separate issue.

Christians who contend that God only loves believers and sees all unbelievers and their good deeds as "filthy rags" may also be stretching the words of Isaiah. In Isaiah 64:6, the prophet was not only voicing God's displeasure with evil acts but pointing out that when compared to His perfection, even the most devoted believers and their best attempts at righteousness fall short. But this is hardly an indictment against the intrinsic value of every human being and all their acts of kindness.

Atheists and agnostics alike have benefited from God's blessings, particularly in the West. Their lives have been completely insulated by the dedication of countless believers who have devoted themselves to improving our quality of life. Even the very freedom they relish to voice their opinions, annoying as they may be, is based on the hard-won concept that all men are created equal and endowed by their Creator with certain inalienable rights.

2. Christian Mind-Reading

Another complaint made against Christians has to do with their sanctimonious tendency to claim knowledge of something they cannot possibly know, namely, what is in another person's head and heart. I have a problem with this myself, because often the standard used for determining, for example, whether or not a person is *saved*, to use a common Christian term, has much more to do with how that person looks or talks than it does with anything else. A person's behavior will render some important clues, however; as Jesus pointed out, "A tree is recognized by its fruit" (Matt. 12:33). But more often than not, subjective rulings tend to be based on variables, such as whether or not a person is a regular church attender, if he or she belongs to the "right" denomination or political party. Or, as far as the more conservative mind thinks, whether or not a person smokes, drinks, uses flowery language, and is pierced or tattooed. If he doesn't use words like, "I asked Jesus into my heart," or if he hasn't responded to an altar call, signed on the dotted line, or begun recommending the Lord to all of his friends, he is immediately suspect. But I often wonder how this leaves room for something as simple as personality differences, levels of understanding, or basic temperaments.

One time, after I spoke at a conference, a woman came up to me and said, "I'm so glad my mother-in-law is here this weekend. She's not a Christian. She's a Catholic." That's quite a declaration, I told her. Unless her mother-in-law has clearly understood the absolute truths of Christ and categorically denied Him (and even then, words can be spoken out of pain or confusion rather than reality), the daughter-in-law is in no position to judge.

I once heard an interview with a priest from Marquette University plugging his book on Milwaukee television. He stated that he was definitely a Christian, but certainly not *born again*. Obviously, not fully understanding the words of Jesus to Nicodemus, "No one can see the kingdom of God unless they are born again" (John 3:3), the author was likely confusing the words of Christ with a conservative Protestant evangelical movement.

3. Fear of the Afterlife

Another common accusation leveled against believers is that religious people created the concept of heaven and the afterlife purely to assuage their fear of death. Theoretical physicist and cosmologist Stephen Hawking was interviewed by Ian Sample of *The Guardian* in 2011. In the article, the science correspondent, referring to Hawking, wrote, "In a dismissal that underlines his firm rejection of religious comforts, Britain's most eminent scientist said there was nothing beyond the moment when the brain flickers for the final time."

Hawking stated, "I regard the brain as a computer which will stop working when its components fail. There is no heaven or afterlife for broken-down computers; that is a fairy story for people afraid of the dark."[1]

Now, clearly, I am no physicist, but from my perspective, this concept is completely backward. Why should we care if there is nothing after this life? We wouldn't know the difference. We'd be gone—components failed. I've been knocked out for surgery and unaware of anything—delightful oblivion. It was upon waking that my troubles began, as I was quickly supplied with a post-op bucket. If I wanted to convince myself that there is nothing after death, I too would make fun of believers, celebrate atheist gatherings, stifle evidence, and attend Darwinian conferences to assure myself that we couldn't *all* be wrong. I'd keep busy too, distracting myself from considering the consequences. But in the end, if I simply cease to exist after I die, so be it. I will have lost nothing having believed there is a God who gives purpose and meaning to life. But the prospect that there might actually be something after death that I'm not prepared for—now *that's* terrifying.

4. A Faith of Convenience

Some charge that the only reason Christians believe in God is because they *want* to believe or simply because that's how they were raised. Again, I've found the opposite to be true. There are plenty of times when being a believer is highly inconvenient, for example, when I'm disappointed with God and how He's doing things, or when I'd rather give a fellow driver something other than a friendly wave. I'd much prefer paganism in these moments. Actress Cloris Leachman believes it's easier. In a 2012 *Huffington Post* interview, she relates a painful story about her grandmother's father who was an Episcopalian minister. When her grandmother was a little girl, her father slapped her in the face for laughing out loud in public. Cloris went on to say, "When I was six years old I heard that God was watching me, and I thought, 'No, no, no, we're not going to have any of that.' And then for many, many years I thought that God would get even with me or punish me because I didn't believe in him, or her, or them. And nothing ever happened except for good things. So I don't believe at all in God, and I'm very relieved that I don't."[2]

Being raised in a particular belief may work for a while, but at some point, we all grow up. In a 2010 *Vogue Magazine* article, supermodel Patti Hansen discussed her health challenges, her faith, and her thirty-year marriage to Keith Richards of the Rolling Stones. "I'm a Christian," she said. "I'm a believer. I believe that Christ is God. And Keith questions all that. I think he believes in a God, but he's not a

Christian. And he just gets into this 'You believe because your parents believed,' and I'll say, 'Don't do that to me, Keith.' I have a strong faith. You are sort of brought into it and then you make a choice yourself. It's my choice."[3] In college, I found that being raised by Christians became a bit of a stumbling block. It seemed unlikely that I should just happen to be born into a home that had an edge on the truth. In fact, there were times when nothing about my parents' church attracted me. I began to wonder if dramatic conversions made it easier to believe or if I could simply stop believing. But it was too late to ignore the weight of the evidence—historical, psychological, and otherwise. The facts wouldn't allow me to disbelieve what I'd already come to believe.

5. Sadistic God

Many atheists and agnostics have accused the God of the Bible of being sadistic. There are probably plenty of Christians who have done the same thing. And maybe this is a sign of the times. Abuses once hidden by closed doors or church hierarchies have been forced open by free-flowing media, including sexual abuse by those who've tried to call themselves men of God. Modern technology and live broadcasting keep us up to date, allowing us an up-close-and-personal look at the devastating consequences of so-called "holy" wars. Furthermore, living in a highly sophisticated, self-sufficient culture has left us a little full of ourselves. We've lost sight of our need for God and His immense holiness. Consequently, we haven't a clue what it means to rightly fear Him or allow Him to make the rules. I've been a little guilty of this myself at times, though I've yet to take it as far as Richard Dawkins, who has described the God of the Bible as a "vindictive, bloodthirsty, ethnic cleanser."[4] Christopher Hitchens branded the Old Testament a mandate toward "indiscriminate massacre."[5]

However, Dr. William Craig is one of many scholars to offer another perspective. He begins by pointing out the irony of our moral sensibilities being offended by the Bible, when many of those sensibilities, including the value of human life, have been largely shaped by our Judeo-Christian heritage. Either way, God's charge to the Israelites to "drive the Canaanites from the land" is unsettling to us—even if God gave them four hundred years to turn from their brutality, bestiality, incest, and child sacrifice. In his book, *Is God a Moral Monster?*, analytic philosopher Paul Copen reminds us that phrases such as, "wipe out every man, woman, and child," represent a kind of hyperbole typical of Ancient Near Eastern accounts of military conquests. In fact, Old Testament scholar Richard Hess points out that there is no record of women or children actually being killed and that all of the battles were with military outposts and soldiers. Whether we attribute the giving and taking of life to a sovereign God who will one day right all wrongs, or whether we believe that existence is a random fluke of evolution and the result of an uncaring universe, the truth remains that good and evil reside on this planet. Personally, when I look around and consider the potential of evil and suffering, I become grateful that of all the frightening ways the eternal God could have chosen to reveal Himself to us, He chose to do so in love.

6. Faith and Science

Questions regarding how the Bible squares with science and evolution are another interesting topic. Even within the church we see a variety of opinions. For example, there are plenty of conservative Bible scholars who hold to a literal interpretation of the book of Genesis and believe in a "young earth" creation story. Many others believe in the message of Genesis but do not take it literally and hold to an "old earth" theory. Still others see Genesis as literal, but are of the old earth opinion, and so on.

There are plenty of scholars in the church today offering their position on these concepts, including the brilliantly articulate mathematician and philosopher of science John Lennox. In his book, *Seven Days That Divide a World,* Lennox, a professor at Oxford University, begins by pointing out that it was the church that became the impetus for scientific research and discovery. Indeed, God's creation is our discovery. But old ideas die slowly, Lennox reminds us, as he considers the reaction to Copernicus and the radical idea that the earth moves.

Change is hard, but whenever we lock our thoughts of God in a box, refusing to remain teachable, no one wins, believers and nonbelievers alike. The Bible is God's revelation of Himself and His character. It reveals His desire for a relationship with those of us who've been placed on this planet, with greater and lesser degrees of accountability being placed on those according to the insight they've been entrusted with. While there is no conflict between science and the Bible, the Bible was never intended to be a science book.

7. Alternative Lifestyle

Another red-hot question in our culture today has to do with whether or not a person can be a Christian and a homosexual at the same time. And by now, I'm pretty sure we've heard just about every kind of answer to this question.

While speaking at a university, Christian apologist Ravi Zacharias handled this issue well, pointing out the fact that no matter how he answered it, he was bound to offend somebody. He reminded his audience that temptation stalks all of us every day. For example, there isn't an able-bodied man among us, he says, who hasn't been physically aroused by the sight of a beautiful woman, even if he is deeply in love with his wife and has no intention of acting out. Some men will struggle with this more than others, and while we could waste a lot of time discussing whether or not they were born that way or conditioned to respond that way, his body is simply reacting to the sight. When this impulse is entertained by the imagination, the urge to act on the temptation will be carried even further. This is true with any sexual impulse, heterosexual and homosexual alike.

Faith in Christ may technically save a person, but choosing to join a church or teach at a particular seminary may take the requirements of their behavior to the next level. As each qualification grows, so does the level of accountability.

Part of our birthright includes deciding what impulses we will nurture and ultimately act upon. Those who choose to engage in homosexuality as a lifestyle are free to do so, at least in our country. Even God Himself allows them that choice. But the pendulum has swung so far in the other direction that it isn't enough for the civil rights of gay people to be protected, as indeed they should be. Gay activists want Christians to completely redesign their concept of marriage, and if they don't, it's the Christian who is the closed-minded bigot, not the gay person. Professor, author, and social critic Camille Paglia is a fascinating, self-described dissident feminist and lesbian who has made some insightful comments pertaining to homosexuality. She has pointed out that Christians have taken a bad rap for standing up against gay marriage. Insomuch as Christians believe the Bible to be God's revealed Word and that He has ordained the union of men and women, calling them bigots or homophobic is unfair. For them, Paglia states, it is a "principled" position in which they are trying to be obedient to God's Word, not unkind to others.

Whether a Christian views homosexuality as a sin or not, the biggest challenge is finding the proper balance, in any issue, of loving the sinner and hating the sin, particularly in light of one's own deficits. Hence, Scripture reminds all of us to take the plank out of our own eye before we criticize the speck in someone else's. When thirteenth-century Italian monk Thomas Aquinas built his arguments for the existence of God on Natural Theology—which argued outside the Bible or morality—he took a stand for heterosexuality in the same way, noting that in the natural order of things, female and male species procreate and perpetuate life. Does this mean we do not see exceptions? No. However, none of this negates the central point about our salvation through Christ.

8. The Problem with Miracles

I often hear people say that the entire story of God and miracles seems both illogical and implausible. And taken at face value, it would seem that way. There is a clever story of a man who went to the doctor complaining that his entire body hurt. The doctor told him to touch his head. "Does that hurt?" the doctor asked him.

"Yes," the man answered.

The doctor said, "Touch your shoulder. Does that hurt?"

"Yes!"

The two continued all the way down the man's body until they reached his feet. The doctor asked, "Does that hurt?"

"Yes!" the man said. "It hurts everywhere I touch."

The doctor replied, "That's because you have a dislocated finger."

Sometimes we need to take a giant step backward before we can move forward. For example, before we even consider the possibility of a miracle, the question that needs to be faced is whether or not we're even open to the possibility that "something" created life. If we are more comfortable thinking that all matter originated from nothing, we'll find it difficult to move to the next question. If we agree that there must be *something* behind existence, then the next question is whether or not we're open to the possibility that that *something* wants to make something of "itself" known. With each step forward, the stakes get higher.

Personally, I think the word *miracle* is overused and, like so many things in our culture, has lost its true meaning. If indeed there is a God who can create life, a miracle would seem to be small potatoes for Him; though that's light years from saying He performs them on a regular basis—which would be a contradiction of terms, as a miracle is defined as not only divine intervention but also an *unusual* event.

Also, the concept of what "seems unusual" is highly subjective. If the apostle Paul had stood on the Acropolis two thousand years ago and told the great minds of his day that one day a man would be able to stand in the same spot and speak face to face to men on the other side of the world simultaneously, they would have responded in anger: "Impossible! Illogical! Delusional! We don't believe in miracles." Those whom Paul addressed in the book of Acts were hardly ignorant. They were the sophisticated minds of their day, yet they would have been unable to imagine something called Skype—which makes me wonder how many other things we might be missing purely because our minds won't budge. Skype was originated by two Scandinavian men, then purchased by Microsoft in 2011. How much more could be invented by the Originator of time and space or energy and matter?

9. One Way to God

Another objection skeptics have is aimed at the narrow-minded position Christians take on Jesus being the only way to God. As I've wrestled long and hard with this one myself, however, I've come to some liberating conclusions. First of all, let's agree that if there is a God, He has the right to make the rules. That makes Him God. Also, when grappling with these kinds of questions, I've realized that, again, our problems are rarely with the truth, but rather our handling of the truth. Have our personal or corporate biases, our perceptions, our traditions, our denominations, and so on somehow locked us into believing something God's Word doesn't say? The real question for me isn't whether or not everyone who is "saved" is saved through Christ, but rather, is it fair for those who haven't heard or understood the message of Christ to be judged for their misfortune? Again, Dr. William Lane Craig's comments are incredibly insightful.

> For according to the Bible, God does not judge people who have never heard of Christ on the basis of whether they have placed their faith in Christ. Rather God judges them on the basis of light of God's general revelation in nature and conscience that they do have. The offer of Romans 2:7 "to those

who by patience in well-doing seek for glory and honor and immortality, He will give eternal life" is a bona fide offer of salvation. This is not to say that people can be saved apart from Christ. Rather it is to say that the benefits of Christ's atoning death could be applied to people without their conscious knowledge of Christ.[6]

This opens up a troublesome can of worms for some Christians but liberates others. Nowhere does Dr. Craig deny that those who are saved are saved through Christ. I also don't see him embracing universalism or the fact that all will be saved in the end. What he is saying is that while all salvation ultimately comes through Christ, it may look different for those who've had different experiences. Dr. Craig points out that it's also very possible that there will be those who are saved without fully knowing how or why. God is just that big.

When I shared these thoughts with my niece and her husband, she said, "Somehow I knew this to be true already but never understood it so clearly or could explain it to someone. It takes care of the gray area that trips people up about Christ being the 'only way' and just further shows how loving and merciful God truly is and how Christ is the key whether you like it or not!"

10. Closed-Mindedness

The most challenging aspect of asking any question is remaining open-minded about the answer. Recognizing how we are influenced by our worldview is essential too. In a debate between Christian apologist William Lane Craig and atheist philosopher Christopher Hitchens, I saw a great example of this. The first man looked at the cosmos and saw evidence of fine-tuning, design, and beauty. The second saw the destruction of shooting stars, collapsed suns, and failed galaxies. The first man contended that Naturalists can dance around it, but the fact remains that there is no empirical evidence that something comes from nothing; a fact he seems less threatened by than the Naturalists. The second man, however, said that if the cosmos is attributed to some sort of creator, then that creator would appear to be capricious, cruel, mysterious, and incompetent.

I've lived on this planet just long enough to realize how difficult it is to stay open-minded and teachable on any subject—a problem that without some effort doesn't appear to improve with age. How much easier it is to dispute others' claims by simply labeling them idiots. Another member of the New Atheist club, Sam Harris, loves to diminish people who disagree with him. He does an amazing job of taking the worst examples of any group and holding them up as the norm. Attractive, articulate, and well dressed, he elevates himself by masterfully reducing others. Michael Moore's documentaries have won prestigious awards for essentially doing the same thing with tremendous artistic flare. But pointing out flaws in any system, ideology, or person is like shooting fish in a barrel. Resorting to terms such as *closed-minded, ignorant,* and *irrational* may be useful for those who are easily swayed and not looking for real answers. But for those who think things through, name-calling becomes little more than an annoying distraction.

However, atheists and other unbelievers are not the only ones who have earned the label *closed-minded.* More than one Christian has earned the label, generally because they are white-knuckle-clinging to an opinion about some interpretation of the Bible. Whether it's a problem with hairstyles, dress codes, marriage and divorce, or even evolution, some believers have completely forgotten about grace and the fact that they may not have a corner on all absolute truth. God is, after all, a bit outside our human understanding. And it wouldn't be all bad if those Christians just clung to their opinion for themselves. The problem comes when they foist their loud objections on the rest of the world.

Sound knowledge should be everyone's pursuit. And to remain open-minded and teachable is the only way to genuinely learn. I used to be afraid to test every theory and truth-claim I held, but I've learned two things along my journey. The first is that, invariably, there are at least two sides to every argument, and we need to listen. The second is that everyone has something to learn. Always. Deliberately clearing through our personal prejudices and preconceived notions is easier said than done. But it's also the only way anyone can secure information that's actually worth having.

Suggested Resources

reasonablefaith.org (Apologist William Lane Craig)
rzim.org (Apologist Ravi Zacharias)
johnlennox.org (Apologist John Lennox)
tellingthetruth.org (Biblical Teaching)
newlife.com (Counseling Network)
annsullivansimpletruths.com (Ann C. Sullivan)

Notes

Chapter 1: Defining Truth
1. Mark 9:24.

Chapter 3: Spiritual Doubt
1. Os Guinness, *God in the Dark: The Assurance of Faith Beyond a Shadow of Doubt* (Wheaton, IL: Crossway, 1996), 13.
2. Matthew S. Stanford, *Grace for the Afflicted: Viewing Mental Illness Through the Eyes of Faith* (Colorado Springs: Paternoster, 2008), 9.

Chapter 4: He Speaks
1. J. V. Langmead Casserley, *The Christian in Philosophy* (New York: Scribner, 1951), 21.

Chapter 7: Is There a God?
1. Steve Rose, "Brad Pitt Talks About Terrence Malick and the Tree of Life," *The Guardian*, June 30, 2011, http://www.theguardian .com/film/2011/jun/30/brad-pitt-interview-terrence-malick.
2. Cynthia Carbone, "Jackson Browne: Even More True Now," *Still Amazed* website, accessed July 8, 2014, http://www.cynthiacar bone.com/zacate/interviews/even-more-true-now-an-interview -with-jackson-browne/.
3. Blaise Pascal, 1670, *Pensées*, translated by W. F. Trotter (London: Dent, 1910), note 233.
4. David Van Biema, "God vs. Science," *Time* (November 5, 2006), http://content.time.com/time/magazine/article/0,9171,1555132 -1,00.html.
5. "Jennifer Michael Hecht Interview," *TBS: The Best Schools* website,

accessed July 8, 2014, http://www.thebestschools.org/features/jen
nifer-michael-hecht-interview/.

Chapter 8: Is Jesus God?
1. Josh McDowell, *Answers to Tough Questions Skeptics Ask About the Christian Faith* (Carol Stream, IL: Tyndale, 1986), 72.
2. C.S. Lewis, *Mere Christianity* (1952; San Francisco: Harper Collins, 2001), 52.

Chapter 9: Is the Bible God's Word?
1. F. F. Bruce, *The New Testament Documents: Are They Reliable?* (Downers Grove, IL: InterVarsity, 1981), 10.
2. David Rim, "Question and Answer," *Today in the Word* 26, no. 4 (April 2013).

Chapter 10: Emotional Doubt
1. C. S. Lewis, *Mere Christianity* (1952; San Francisco: Harper Collins, 2001).
2. C. S. Lewis, *A Grief Observed* (London: Faber, 1961), 48.

Chapter 12: Fueling the Flames with Anxiety and Depression
1. See the U.S. Population Clock at United States Census Bureau, http://www.census.gov/.
2. "Anxiety Disorders: Who Is at Risk," National Institute of Mental Health, accessed July 8, 2014, http://www.nimh.nih.gov/health/topics/anxiety-disorders/index.shtml#part4.

Chapter 13: Changing the Way We Think
1. Claire Weekes, *Hope and Help for Your Nerves* (New York: Hawthorn Books, 1969).
2. Norman Vincent Peale, *The Power of Positive Thinking* (New York: Simon and Schuster, 1952), 6.

Chapter 15: Rethinking Doubt

1. J. I. Packer, *Evangelism and the Sovereignty of God* (Downers Grove, IL: InterVarsity, 1961), 19.

Appendix: Ten Reasons Not to Be a Christian

1. "Stephen Hawking: 'There Is No Heaven; It's a Fairy Story,'" *The Guardian* (May 15, 2011), http://www.theguardian.com/science/2011/may/15/stephen-hawking-interview-there-is-no-heaven.

2. Debra Ollivier, "Cloris Leachman: On 'Raising Hope,' Growing Up, and Believing (Or Not) in God," *Huffington Post* (June 20, 2012), http://www.huffingtonpost.com/debra-ollivier/cloris-leachman-raising-hope_b_1606927.html.

3. Jonathan Van Meter, "Patti Hansen: Rock Steady," *Vogue Magazine*, July 15, 2010, http://www.vogue.com/magazine/article/patti-hansen-rock-steady/#1.

4. Richard Dawkins, *The God Delusion* (New York: Mariner, 2006), 51.

5. Christopher Hitchens, *God Is Not Great: How Religion Poisons Everything* (New York: Twelve, 2007), 102.

6. William Lane Craig, "How Can Christ Be the Only Way to God?" *Reasonable Faith with William Lane Craig*, accessed May 23, 2014, http://www.reasonablefaith.org/how-can-christ-be-the-only-way-to-god.